D0975854

ORGANIZATIONAL CONSULTING:
A Gestalt Approach

Organizational Consulting

A GESTALT APPROACH

Edwin C. Nevis

Gestalt Institute of Cleveland Press
Published and Distributed by
GARDNER PRESS, INC., New York, London

Gestalt Institute of Cleveland Press
Published and Distributed by Gardner Press

GARDNER PRESS, INC.
19 UNION SQUARE WEST
NEW YORK, NEW YORK 10003

All foreign orders except Canada and South America to:
Afterhurst Limited
Chancery House
319 City Road
London, N1, United Kingdom

Library of Congress Cataloging-in-Publication Data

Nevis, Edwin C.
Organizational Consulting.
Includes index.
1. Gestalt therapy. 2. Organizational effectiveness—
Psychological aspects. 3. Consultants. I. Title.
[DNLM: 1. Psychotherapy—methods. 2. Referral and
Consultation. WM 420 N521o]
RC489.G4N48 1987 616.89′143 85-20555
ISBN 0-89876-124-7

Design by Publishers Creative Services

In Memory of
Richard W. Wallen
—Teacher, Colleague, Friend

Contents

Preface

The subject of this book is the sequence of becoming aware and turning this awareness into useful action. I see the major objective of consulting relationships as being the education of the client system in how to improve its awareness of its functioning and to enhance its ability to take actions that improve this functioning. By awareness I mean the knowing or cognizance that derives from observation of self or other. The process of being aware is simply that of using all of the senses in an alert, attentive way. Through our senses—seeing, hearing, feeling, smelling—we become conscious of what is happening to us and around us. This realization provides the energy and direction for action and learning. Influential process consultation depends on how well the helping professional uses his or her awareness in making useful interventions in work systems.

An effective awareness process helps the consultant to deal with all stages of intervention, from entry and grounding to resolution and completion of the work. Achievement of this goal requires a high level of skill in becoming aware of self and of what is happening in the client system. Awareness forms a basis for the use of self as an instrument of change; it provides the potential for one's presence to have a high impact. The effective consultant draws power from awareness and teaches client systems to do likewise. The special value of the Gestalt orientation lies in the way in which the awareness process is conceptualized in the Gestalt Cycle of Experience, and in its emphasis on high-contact ("strong presence") process consultation. This book describes how I have extended this model to use it in organization consulting.

The thinking expressed here stems from the perspective of an organization consultant who has learned much from Gestalt therapy but is not a practicing therapist in the classical sense.

I became a consultant first, then I studied Gestalt therapy. During my early years of practice, I worked from two assumptions concerning the role of the organization consultant: scientifically based, objective data gathering is the service to be provided and Rogerian nondirective counseling is the best framework for consultant–client interactions. Implicit in these assumptions is an underlying belief that the feelings, emotions, fantasies, images, and other personal experiences of the consultant, are detrimental to the work with clients if not held under control. As with most other therapeutic approaches that prevailed up to the early 1950s, it was assumed that theory and methodology were more important than the way in which the intervenor used personal experiences to achieve a compelling, unique presence. However, the studies I began with Fritz Perls and others enabled me to experience the power of personal, here-and-now, subjective experience as a support for the work of the consultant. It became apparent that a more potent consulting style might be developed through use of the Cycle of Experience and Gestalt methods of high-contact interaction.

From 1959 to 1971, I was a senior partner in an organization consulting firm and also served as president of the Gestalt Institute of Cleveland. During the first seven years of this period, I studied with Fritz Perls, Laura Perls, Isadore From, Paul Goodman, Erving Polster, and family therapists of related orientation, such as Carl Whitaker and Virginia Satir. Additional significant learning came from the good fortune of having Richard W. Wallen as a colleague from 1957 until his untimely death in 1968. Not only was he one of the greatest teachers of his time, but his interest in experimentation and his courage led us to use Gestalt awareness methods with managers as early as 1959.

The reader will note that emphasis is placed more on concepts and frameworks than on detailed case presentations of full consulting assignments. Examples and brief cases from my own practice are offered, but these are used mainly to illustrate the models and insights that have driven my work. I believe that we need more articulation from practitioners as to their guiding principles and values, and that effective consultation requires a coherent theoretical framework.

The ideas expressed herein were fostered and developed during my long association with colleagues at the Gestalt Institute of Cleveland, and credit must be shared with Bill Warner, Erving Polster, Sonia Nevis, Joseph Zinker, Elaine Kepner, Marjorie Creelman, Cynthia Harris, Rainette Fantz, and Miriam Polster—all of whom are clinical psychologists or psychiatrists. My application to organizations of their work at the individual or family level was aided greatly by my association since 1973 with the staff of the Cleveland Institute's program in Organization and System Development: Carolyn Lukensmeyer, John Carter, Elaine Kepner, Claire Stratford, Leonard Hirsch, and Jeffrey Voorhees. Several of the chapters were first developed as lecture outlines for this program.

My ideas were further tested and refined over the past seven years of teaching seminars in theories of change and the management of planned change at the Sloan School of Management of the Massachusetts Institute of Technology. I am very grateful to Richard Beckhard and Edgar Schein for making it possible for me to present and develop my thinking in this environment. The excitement of students who had little or no knowledge of Gestalt therapy convinced me that a wider audience would appreciate this work.

A word of thanks is due David Monroe Miller and Marvin Weisford who furnished detailed reviews of the first draft of this book. Their feedback and suggestions were invaluable. I hope they can see their influence in these pages.

Finally, I wish to acknowledge the enormous support of my wife, Sonia M. Nevis, for the development of my ideas and my writing. As my warm and incisive conversational partner for many years, she helped me to be consistent with Gestalt theory and clear in expressing myself. This would be a much poorer statement without her involvement.

1
Development and Application of the Gestalt Figure–Ground Model

The perspective to be elaborated on in this book stems from the theory and practice of Gestalt therapy as it has developed since first presented by Fritz Perls, Paul Goodman, Laura Perls, and Isadore From in the 1940s (Perls, 1947; Perls et al., 1951). This approach derived largely out of an attempt to integrate into psychoanalytic theory the findings of the Gestalt studies of perception and learning by Wertheimer (1945), Koffka (1922, 1935), and Kohler (1927, 1929, 1947); the related work of Kurt Lewin (1935, 1951a) and Kurt Goldstein (1939); and work by other phenomenological and existential thinkers. The major thrust of the early work was supported by Perls' attack upon what he considered to be gaps or errors in the Freudian model, and was oriented essentially to individual development and the treatment of neurosis in the individual. Since then students of Perls and his early associates have worked with the concepts and methods and have applied them to systems of more than one person. In the course of 30 years at the Gestalt Institute of Cleveland, the awareness process that is the basis of Gestalt therapy became identified as the *Gestalt Cycle of Experience* ("Cycle"). Figures 1-1, 1-2 present the Cycle in diagrammatic form.

The Cycle summarizes the process by which people—individually or collectively—become *aware* of what is going on at any moment, and how they mobilize *energy* to take some *ac-*

tion that allows them to deal constructively with possibilities suggested by the new awareness. This process is sometimes simply referred to as that of finding out what is needed and going about getting it. It assumes that when a disequilibrium in the state of being or functioning of a person(s) comes into awareness, the natural human tendency is to want to do something to achieve a new state of equilibrium. The model also assumes that there is an inherent desire in people to function at the most effective, satisfying level possible, and that learning to utilize this process is a key to the achievement of optimum functioning. Finally, the model assumes that the process results in a culminating experience that can be seen as learning or that which derives from the meaning of the experience. This stage of the Cycle is referred to as *resolution* or *closure*.

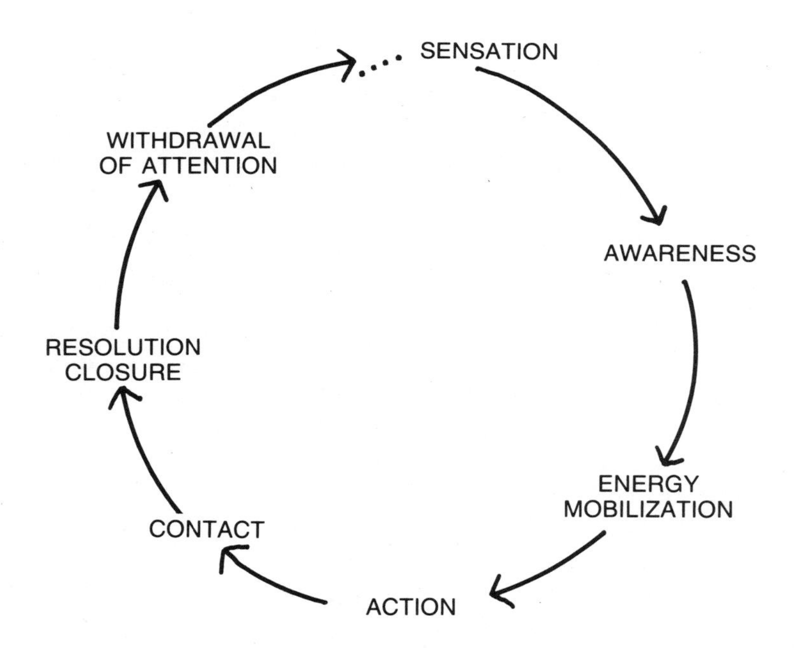

Figure 1-1. Gestalt Cycle of Experience: Flow of a unit of uninterrupted experience

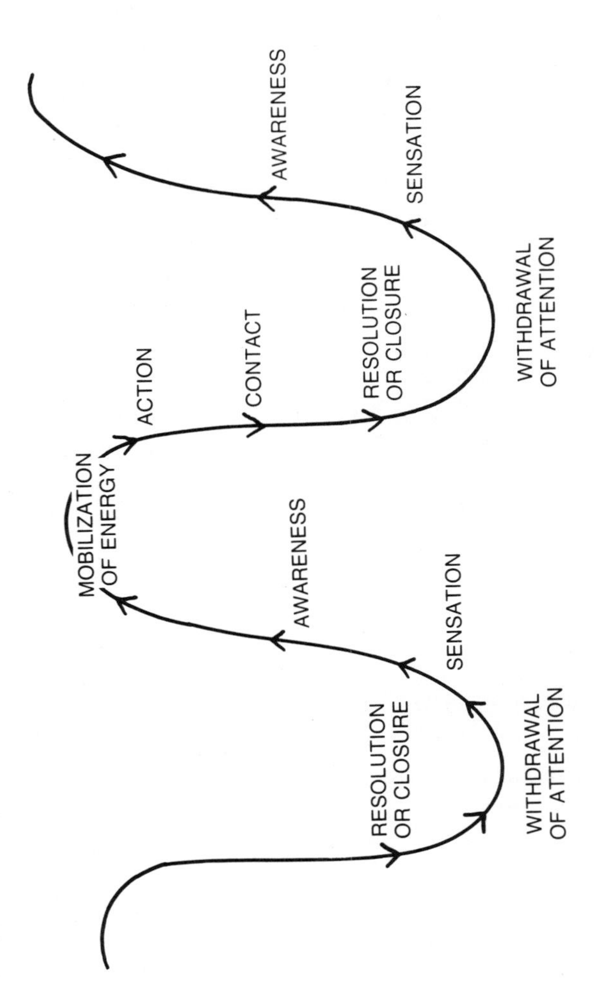

Figure 1-2. Flow of Continuous Experience

The Gestalt Cycle of Experience integrates the behavioral aspects of sensation, awareness, energy mobilization, contact, and resolution or closure into a complete unit of human experience. The ability of individuals and human systems to move smoothly through the phases of the Cycle is considered essential for healthy functioning and learning. When an individual or group develops heightened awareness of what is needed at a given moment, mobilizes energy to get it, and can then fully assimilate knowledge from this sequence of behavior, we say that healthy human process has taken place. Within this perspective, the role of the helping professional is to assist people to become more effective in performing this behavioral sequence. Use of the Cycle as an orienting principle is one of the major distinguishing features of a Gestalt-oriented consultant or therapist.

A second orienting principle of Gestalt therapy in the consulting mode is that the use of the self in high-contact interactions with clients helps to promote learning and growth. Gestalt consulting involves an active, strong *presence* on the part of the consultant; presence is a major support in the modeling of and the teaching of the Cycle of Experience. This orienting principle will be elaborated in later chapters, after the Cycle has been discussed in some detail.

EARLY STUDIES OF VISUAL PERCEPTION

In order to understand the Cycle of Experience, it may help to review some aspects of Gestalt psychology that are basic to Gestalt therapy. Gestalt psychology was developed in Germany early in the 20th century by Max Wertheimer (1945), Wolfgang Kohler (1927, 1929), Kurt Koffka (1922, 1935), and Kurt Lewin (1935, 1951).* It is predicated upon the belief that complex human behavior cannot be explained as an additive building up of simple components. According to the Gestalt psychologists, experience does not come out of the accumulation or association of fundamental behavioral "atoms"; the true data of experience

*Hilgard (1948) and Smith (1976) present good short reviews of this work.

are organized wholes. For example, in looking at Figure 1-3, people see only a square; later they may "break it down" as being composed of four equal lines attached to each other at 90-degree angles.

Gestalt psychologists showed that the world of sensory data is arranged in an organized manner, and that people react to the overall pattern or unitary organization of objects, not to specific bits or parts. They called the perceived patterns *Gestalten*, or configurations, and studied how they formed and changed. In numerous experiments, including some by Kohler with adults who were born blind and later gained sight, it was shown that the perception of form is an inherent human quality. Objects are seen as organized or as having coherent, "given" arrangements even though people may not have names for them. Moreover, this is not simply a passive response; people work actively to impose order upon what they see.

The early work of the Gestalt psychologists was largely concerned with visual perception. Out of these studies emerged some important principles, perhaps the most basic being that of the figure-ground relationship. Each gestalt is seen as a figure

Figure 1-3. A square composed of four three-inch lines connected to form 90-degree angles.

that stands out against a vaguer background. The figure has clear form, while the background, or ground, tends to be less clearly formed. The figure is more interesting, has more meaning attributed to it, and remains in memory better than the ground. In fact, as the Danish psychologist Rubin showed, figures tend to resist change once they are formed. People will likely see later just about what they saw in earlier perceptions of objects, a phenomenon that promotes rigidity and makes it difficult to look at something familiar from a fresh viewpoint.

A figure develops through the focusing of attention; the process is called gestalt formation, or figure formation. An example of figure formation would be to have one's attention drawn to an interesting tree while walking through a wooded park. As the tree is seen more and more clearly and vividly, it becomes "singled out"—differentiated—from the general background.

FIGURE FORMATION

Figure or gestalt formation is a process by which we see the whole first, then we break it down or differentiate the parts. The whole is more than the sum of the parts, as the arrangement or configuration of the parts is what gives an object its unique quality. In the case of singling out a tree in a park, the object is perceived almost immediately as a tree even if our attention is drawn to some parts more than to others. Studying only isolated, single parts of the tree (trunk, roots, branches, leaves, etc.) does not allow one to experience that which we call "tree." If any part of the tree were to change, such as the leaves turning brown, we would still see the object as a tree.

To form a figure is to become interested in or concerned about something and to strive to give meaning to the experience. Being in touch with a figure as it forms is what we call "'awareness." This is our way of taking in what our senses tell us and of knowing what is happening at any moment. This is the beginning phase of the Cycle of Experience.

Several features of figure formation are highly relevant to an understanding of the awareness process in general, and to the work of the organizational consultant in particular. To begin with, receptivity, or the ability to allow objects to differentiate out of a varied, rich, or complex background, is essential. One is not able either to take in the wooded quality of a park or to single out and appreciate a particular tree without being open to stimuli that create experience. One can easily walk through a park while being engaged in deep thought and not notice the existence of trees. In other words, the ability to see, hear, smell, taste, and/or feel must be available in order for any object to become interesting. We can think of this interaction of our senses and the external or internal world as simply a way of learning about the world, or of being in touch with our existence so that we can find out what we need at any given moment, and then go about getting it. Wandering around in our environment without a particular direction or goal enables us to maintain an unjudgmental posture. It allows for one or more of our senses to become aroused and for our interest to grow in response. This is what happens whenever we discover something new or fresh, and it is the way in which unforeseen or serendipitous learning may occur. It is the basic process of awareness that underlies the practice of "management by wandering around" (MBWA) that Peters and Waterman discuss in *In Search of Excellence* (1982). In this practice managers place themselves in a receptive frame by spending a great deal of undirected, open-focused time in the work units for which they are responsible. They manage by responding to the figures that emerge during that experience.

On the other hand, to allow our senses full play—to become broadly and deeply aware of something—requires concentration beyond receptivity, and involves the motoric, as well as the sensory, system. The process of attending to something in order to know it in full measure is real work. Receptivity is both an active and a passive process. In this regard it is interesting to note that Perls originally called his approach "concentration therapy" to highlight the fact that his methods were designed to help people learn to direct their energy toward the process of attending to their external and internal worlds. In daily life we do not ordinarily stop to consider that attending is work, but we constantly make choices as to what to attend to, and how much time and energy to devote to anything that begins to emerge as figural in our awareness. For example:

> I walked on a seashore road in Cape Cod where I had walked for over 20 years. My attention was drawn to a large spider's web dangling from a pine tree by several threads. Ordinarily, I would have continued walking and merely relegated this figure—developed out of a passive receptivity—to my poorly defined and biased taxonomic bin for the experience of spiders and their webs. However, this time I decided to stop and attend further to the web, and to make all else background. I looked at it from the front, back, and side; I walked close to it and then stepped back in order to get perspective from various distances. I realized that the web was more complex than I had noted initially. Among other things, it had many more rings than were seen at first glance, and it had threads that varied in thickness, certain points or junctures that contained a minute, white-colored substance, and it held moisture on the surface of the threads. I concentrated on the web for about five minutes and developed a rich, vivid figure. I then resumed my walk, and the image of the web faded as my attention was directed elsewhere. Gestalt psychologists would say that figure formation and destruction had taken place.

This example illustrates two points. First, I had *worked* at broadening my experience of the spider web by devoting time and energy to its observation. I moved my body, refocused my eyes from time to time, became alternately tense and loose in my stance and motion, and changed my breathing as I became more excited about my observations. Second, I had made choices as to how much and what kind of attention to devote to this study of the web. That is, I only observed it for a short period of time. I did not touch it, feel it, taste it, or put my ear close to it to see if it emitted any sound. The net result was a heightened experience of the spider's web, but certainly not a full knowledge of this web or of webs in general. More work would have been required for fuller appreciation.

LAW OF PRAGNANZ

A second Gestalt principle that is important to Gestalt therapy, and that has significant implication for organization consulting, is the law of Pragnanz, or the law of equilibrium. This principle states that every experience, whether perceptual or of another modality, tends to become as "good" as prevailing stimulus conditions make possible. It is analogous to the notion of equilibrium in physics, and it means that psychological organization is not random, but tends to move in a given, compelling, more stable direction, than in any other direction. The result is the "good" gestalt, which has properties of simplicity, regularity, proximity, and closure.

Closure may be considered a special case of the law of Pragnanz in that it refers to the inherent human tendency to complete incomplete or confused perceptions. The principle of closure states that people strive actively toward completion of perception or action and are not satisfied until they do so. This may be thought of as an equilibrium-producing process. A closed figure is a better figure than an open one, and an incomplete figure can be thought of as an "unfinished situation." As we will see later, one of the major contributions of an organization consultant is to help people learn to deal with unfinished situations around which they are stuck or blocked.

The drawings in Figure 1-4 illustrate the principle of Pragnanz and closure. They call out to be seen as "triangle" and the letter "S," even though we are aware that gaps exist in the shapes. In fact, if we expose these figures quickly on a screen, the gaps are not seen at all. We can also see that completion of these figures is influenced by the rule of simplicity—it would take quite an effort of imagination to see different figures here. Koffka and Kohler performed numerous studies in which they demonstrated that small irregularities in objects are not perceived, and that there is an inherent tendency to see things as symmetrical even when they are not.

EXTENSION TO THE REALM OF MOTIVATION/ACTION

Koffka (1935) saw the law of Pragnanz as a guiding principle for the understanding of how learning takes place, and he conceived the ease or difficulty of a problem as a matter of perception of the field. That is, the development of a correct or use-

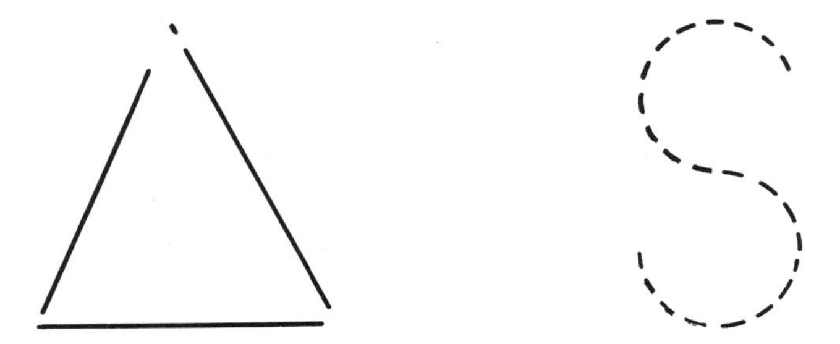

Figure 1-4. Closure: figures are perceived as completed triangle and an "S."

ful response is a function of how well conditions in the field (including both person and environment) enable the law of Pragnanz to function. To the extent that the field is open to the viewer for observations that allow a "best fit" to develop, there will occur an equilibrium-producing response that allows for closure and for an end to the active search of the learner. In problem-solving studies with apes, Kohler (1927) used the term "insight" to refer to this phenomenon when illustrated by the ape learning to put small sticks together in order to reach a banana. This is an example at a more complex behavioral level of the active perception that is implied by the principles of equilibrium (Pragnanz) and closure. At a more complex level, such as managerial problem solving, we can often see a group of managers struggle with a vague or difficult issue, trying to bring order into a confused or chaotic situation. If conditions exist that do not allow "best fit" observations to occur—for example, when a solution persisting from past experiences is so figural that the present field is not seen appropriately, or when important facts and opinions are not available to the group—an improper solution is often selected. Also, there are times when an improper definition of a problem is made. To look for ways to increase quality of a product through improvement in manufacturing methods when the real problem lies in defects in raw material is to structure the field so that a correct response is not forthcoming. The result is that the group might think it has reached closure and has ended its active learning, only to experience later tension and discomfort when quality does not improve. We can refer to this problem as false or premature closure.

The above examples are offered to make the point that the principles of figure formation do not apply only to passive perceptual behavior, but also help to explain more complex behavior. The initial Gestalt psychologists saw gestalt or figure formation as a basic function of how individuals interact with their environment in many situations. How people come to know their world, how learning takes place, and how meaning is given to experience were the issues of study. They did not at first associate their principles with the principles of perception of feelings, emotions, or bodily sensations, or to motivation. It was Kurt Lewin who became interested in the integration of motivational issues with the facts of perception.* He saw a need to add the constructs of energy and tension systems in order to better understand higher-order behavior. In his view organizations of the field, or life-space as he called it, are directed or influenced by intentions that act as though they are needs. Once an intention develops, it creates a tension system in a person; there is energy to do something, to move toward a desired goal.†

Lewin saw intentions as having the quality of quasi-needs, and understood the unfolding process as being very similar to that of satisfying the basic needs of living. To explain how action followed from perception, he concluded that the constructs of energy and balance are necessary: a need arising in someone produces tension that guides or "energizes" the perception of objects in the environment. Activity aroused by need tension systems is guided by perception, and psychological behavior was seen as depending upon energy coming from tension systems. As Lewin (1951b) put it:

> The property of a need or quasi-need can be represented by coordinating it to a "system in tension". . . by correlating the "release of tension" to a "satisfaction of a need" (or the reaching of a goal), and the "setting up of a tension" to an "inten-

*For a discussion of Lewin's model see Heider (1960).

†Actually, Koffka was the first one to use the term "tension" to describe the involvement of the total organism when a desired goal has not yet been reached. He described this as that which changes the relationship between person and environment in such a way that the goal is attained. (1935)

> tion" or a "need in a state of hunger", a great number of testable conclusions were made possible. (pp.5–6)

Lewin showed that needs influence perception in terms of what is seen and of what kind of action then follows to satisfy a need. People do not see just anything, but form figures in support of what they need (if I am hungry, my attention is likely to be drawn to food objects). Moreover, they will move toward objects that can satisfy this need; they do not engage in random behavior once having organized the field in support of an emerging need. A thorough phenomenologist, Lewin also saw that people in the same situation exist in different life-spaces. For instance, people who attend the same meeting are actually in varying psychological worlds. Whether they are attending to different sensory and mental stimuli or having different need tension systems, they will define their internal experience and their experience of the social and physical environment in unique ways.

Lewin viewed behavior as a function of the person–environment interaction as it existed at any given moment. His emphasis upon the "here and now," and upon the organization of the field at the present moment, was a key factor in directing the Gestalt focus away from the study of the past (so crucial to psychoanalysis). He postulated that what has an effect in any given moment is not a past event itself but, rather, the nature of present awareness of that event. Present conditions regulate and redefine past experience and its application to the present moment. The implication of this for the utilization of past learning in the present moment is significant. Application of past perceptions, responses, or solutions that are not coherent with the present field are likely to be inappropriate. Perls underscored this as a particularly critical point, and he developed much of his therapeutic methodology to help people become more aware of the present as it develops from moment to moment. He referred to this as the "awareness continuum," and the methodology emphasizes the loosening of "fixed gestalts"—figures developed out of past experience that become adhered to rigidly in the present situation. By achieving greater clarity of awareness of the present situation, one sees how and in what way past learning may be utilized.

A related line of work by Lewin and his students concerns unfinished situations, those instances where an intention has been roused but which, for one reason or another, the resulting tension system has not been allowed to lead to fulfillment of the need, or to closure. In a series of experiments by Zeigarnik (1938) and Ovsiankina (1976), it was shown that memory for incompleted or interrupted tasks is greater than memory for finished tasks by a factor of at least two or three times. Lewin saw the finished task as completed gestalt, with tension relieved through attainment of a goal and fulfillment of an intention. Such completion can be considered as an illustration of the law of Pragnanz in action. On the other hand, the incompleted task—the unfinished situation—has created an unfulfilled tension and leaves the person unsatisfied due to lack of closure. (Other theories refer to this residue of physiological and mental activity as perseveration.) Examples of the phenomenon abound in everyday life: the unsolved problem that holds our continuous attention while it remains unsolved; the unexpressed feelings that are aroused but that cannot be expressed; an interesting event that, while its meaning eludes us, is recalled from time to time.

EXTENSION TO TOTAL ORGANISMIC FUNCTIONING

Movement from the study of perception to a broader definition of the realm of Gestalt psychology was further aided by the work of Kurt Goldstein (1939), who developed many of his insights from work with brain-damaged soldiers in Germany during World War I. Goldstein, like other Gestalt psychologists, saw the figure-ground paradigm as a basic concept, but he extended it to stand for the process of total organismic functioning. Starting with his observation of the ways in which brain-damaged persons managed to shift impaired functions to undamaged parts of the brain, he generalized his studies to normal people and to the development of a more refined view of what he called "holistic" organismic process. He conceptualized different levels of human functioning, regarding basic tension reduction mechanisms, such as responses to threat or physical need, as a lower order of functioning than the process of finding out what one wants and getting it. The latter was seen as a more assertive, manipulative interaction with the environment. This, in turn, was perceived as a less complex process than the overriding motive of striving to become all that one is capable of being, which he called "self-actualization." These levels are related through dynamic process in which tensions continually occur as needs at one level are satisfied. Once deficiency/threat needs—such as the need to repair brain-damaged functions or to obtain food when hungry—are satisfied, the human organism turns to another level of concern or interest. Thus Goldstein postulated that satisfaction of needs at any level provides direct awareness of (makes figural) other needs or goals signifying worthwhile higher achievements. In fact, Goldstein believed that it was necessary only to postulate one need level, that of self-actualization, to account for a wide variety of important personality and motivational phenomena.*

APPLICATION TO INDIVIDUAL DEVELOPMENT

Perls connected the fixed Gestalt and the unfinished situation as being powerful determinants of the individual's inability to form fresh, new figures in the present moment. He saw that hanging on to past perceptions of people or events prevented comprehension of what would be the most useful behavior in the "here and now." By carrying around tensions from unfinished past experiences, one ties up energy and is unable to make good contact with the person(s) or object(s) that are the focal point of the unfinished business. He realized that people cannot have appropriate interactions until tensions derived from the past are released in some way. His technique of having an

*Maslow's "hierarchy of needs" formulation derives directly from this, including his borrowing of the term "self-actualization" (Maslow, 1954).

individual talk to a nonpresent other by imagining the other to be seated in an empty chair was seen as a way of operationalizing movement toward some kind of closure in the present.

As an assistant to Goldstein for a short period, Perls was highly influenced by his ideas, particularly the notion that organismic self-regulation provides an autonomous criterion of good health. One had mainly to learn how to be able to get in touch with needs and wants, and then to satisfy them, in order to be considered a well-functioning person. Moreover, Fritz Perls, Laura Perls, and Paul Goodman believed that the task of therapy is not simply to relieve people of burdensome feelings and attitudes, such as low self-esteem and guilt, but to embrace broader objectives. For them the ultimate goal is to teach not only need satisfaction but also how to move in the world: to talk, walk, relate, and so forth, with fluidity, grace, and dignity. Trained in music and dance, Laura Perls intuitively included the general stance and use of the body as a subject of self-development.* Paul Goodman, with his strong passion for social change, extended the realm to include how one behaved in the community. In this way the basic figure-ground model was broadened to include the full spectrum of individual–environment relationships. Awareness was seen as the foundation of the developmental process, and Gestalt therapy might well be called "human learning based on the Gestalt figure-ground model."

Once the focus was directed to all aspects of how people find out what they need from their environment and how they go about getting it, the laws of progressive Gestalt formation and destruction were accepted as providing an automatic, value-free criterion of adjustment. Appropriate, healthy behavior is that which enables people to recognize what they need at any given moment, and to obtain it. A healthy, well-integrated person is one in whom this process goes on constantly; unhealthy manifestation (resistances) are seen as interruptions of the pro-

---

*Both Fritz and Laura Perls were influenced by the body armor theory of Wilhelm Reich (1949), with whom Fritz Perls underwent psychoanalysis for a period of time. Fritz Perls was also intrigued by Moreno's work in the theater and with role playing, using this as a taking-off point for improvisation in the therapeutic setting.

cess. Richard Wallen (1970) has summarized the centrality of this point:

> The importance of this process for biological survival should be evident, for only as the individual is able to extract from the environment those things he needs to survive, in order to feel comfortable and interested in the world around him, will he actually be able to live on both a biological and psychological level. We cannot feed off ourselves: we cannot breathe without breathing in the environment; we cannot do anything to take into our bodies those necessary things we require, whether it is affection, knowledge, or air, without interacting with the environment. Consequently, the clarity of this relationship that I have tried to describe, Gestalt formation and destruction, becomes of the utmost importance for the individual's living.

REFINEMENT OF INDIVIDUAL THERAPY

Since the early 1950s, Gestalt therapy has been employed by practitioners all over the world. Numerous institutes and teaching centers have enhanced the theory and method in various ways. The Cycle of Experience is but one of the extensions of the basic awareness model formulated in the early writings. Advances in technique have also followed, as experienced therapists have refined their work over the years. Other experiential therapists are now popular. Some people have integrated such techniques as body therapies, hypnosis, and Jungian concepts, into their use of Gestalt therapy.

There is a substantial body of literature now available on Gestalt therapy with individuals. (See Polster & Polster, 1973; Zinker, 1977; Fagan & Shepherd, 1970; Pursglove, 1968; Latner, 1973; Wysong & Rosenfeld, 1982, the *Gestalt Journal*; *Voices*, etc.) For the present purpose, suffice it to say that the figure-ground model remains the paradigm for those who continue to work within this framework. In Chapter 2. the Cycle of Experience is presented as a way of keeping the basic awareness model constantly in mind while working. This conception has had many years of use in individual therapy.

APPLICATION TO LARGER SYSTEMS

The first applications in larger systems were those in which Gestalt methodology was used with individuals in organizational settings. Beginning in 1959, Richard W. Wallen and the author applied awareness techniques to sensitivity training in order to explore ways of aiding individuals to see themselves more clearly and to make better contact with others. This general approach to individual development has been documented by Herman and Korenich (1977), and has since been expanded to team building and third-party interventions. This work includes the undoing of projections that interfere with a clear perception of self and other, the expression and utilization of feelings in decision making, and the use of fantasy and experiment. As with the early teaching of Gestalt therapy to helping professionals, these applications have almost always employed a group or workshop format and are seen as educational interventions.

A parallel line of development is application to work with couples and families. As the focus of therapy has shifted from individuals to larger units, so has the use of Gestalt therapy. The work of Kempler (1974), S. Nevis and Zinker (1982), William Warner, C. Wesley Jackson, and others is well known, and their writings, as well as those of their students, are now beginning to appear. It was out of work at the family level that Zinker and Nevis (1981) conceived of the "Gestalt Interactive Cycle," a concept discussed in detail in Chapter 2. Patricia Papernow has applied the Cycle of Experience to the problems of step-parenting and combining families (1984).

A third level of application has been to larger systems, particularly to organizations. Most of this work has been geared toward the consultant process, as elaborated in this volume. However, a number of people have been impressed with possible linkages between Gestalt therapy and systems theory (see Burke, 1980 and Latner, 1983). Finally, Merry and Brown (1987) have described and studied neurotic organizational behavior from the viewpoint of the concepts of Gestalt therapy.

SUMMARY

The basic theoretical underpinnings of Gestalt therapy and of the Gestalt consulting approach described herein were derived from a model of perception that was extended to motivational phenomena and, later, to the process of total organismic functioning. Fundamental to this orientation is the principle of the figure-ground relationship and the law of Pragnanz. Application of these principles to various aspects of human behavior leads to a process conception of good functioning that emphasizes the value of awareness of self and other in the present moment. Particular attention is given to finding out what is needed to adapt to the changing situation as individuals relate to each other and to their environment. An underlying assumption of this conception is that human action is a self-regulating system that deals with an unstable state in such a way as to produce a state of stability. The process is seen as being more than deficiency alleviation; it embraces the higher-order functions of growth and creative behavior. Fritz Perls and his early associates developed these precepts into a method of therapy oriented to the task of helping people to be more effective in this process. This method calls for the helping professional to use him or herself in a highly involved way, as contact between the helper and the client system is seen as critical to the actualization of effective awareness process.

While much of the work with Gestalt theory has been directed toward understanding and helping the individual, it has also been applied to groups, families, and organizations. It has provided an extremely useful orientation to therapeutic and consulting work at all levels. For teaching and practice purposes, the faculty of the Gestalt Institute of Cleveland has summarized the process as the Gestalt Cycle of Experience. Table 1-1 sum-

Table 1-1. Summary of the Development and Application of the Gestalt Figure-Ground Model

1. Early studies of visual perception
    - The figure-ground relationship
    - Law of Pragnanz/closure
    - Insight learning (Wertheimer, Koffka, Kohler)
2. Extension to the realm of motivation/action
    - Intentions, tension systems
    - Importance of the here and now
    - Unfinished situations (Kurt Lewin and students)
3. Extension to total organismic functioning
    - Organismic self-regulation
    - Principle of self-actualization
    - Holism (Kurt Goldstein and students)
4. Application to individual development
    - Awareness training
    - Methods for here-and-now therapy
    - Treatment of the whole person
      (F. Perls, L. Perls, P. Goodman, I. From, New York Institute of Gestalt Therapy)
5. Refinement of individual therapy
    - Gestalt Cycle of Experience
    - Integration with other approaches to human development
      (Faculties of Gestalt Institute of Cleveland and other institutes, practicing therapists)
6. Application to larger systems
    - Couples and family therapy
      (W. Warner, S. Nevis, J. Zinker, W. Jackson, W. Kempler, Center for Intimate Systems)
    - Individual development in organizational roles
      (R. Wallen, E. Nevis, S. Herman, and M. Korenich)
    - Organizational consulting
      (E. Nevis, L. Hirsch, J. Carter, C. Lukensmeyer, E. Kepner, C. Stratford, J. Voorhees, W. Burke, U. Merry, G. Brown)

marizes the historical progression of thought from the initial Gestalt psychologists to the present application.

REFERENCES

Burke, W.W. "Systems theory, Gestalt therapy, and organization development." In T.G. Cummings (ed.), *Systems Theory for Organization Development*. London: Wiley, 1980.

Fagan, J., and Sheperd, I. *Gestalt Therapy Now.* Palo Alto: Science and Behavior Books, 1970.

Goldstein, K. *The Organism.* New York: American Book Co., 1939.

Heider, F. "The Gestalt theory of motivation." In M. Jones, (ed.), *Nebraska Symposium on Motivation: 1960.* Lincoln: University of Nebraska Press, 1960.

Herman, S.M., and Korenich, M. *Authentic Management.* Reading, Mass.: Addison-Wesley, 1977.

Hilgard, E. *Theories of Learning.* New York: Appleton-Century-Crofts, 1948.

Kempler, W. *Principles of Gestalt Family Therapy.* Oslo: Nordahls Taykkeri, 1974.

Koffka, K. "Perception: An introduction to the Gestalt theory." *Psychology Bulletin,* 1922, 19, 531–585.

Koffka, K. *Principles of Gestalt Psychology.* New York: Harcourt, Brace, 1935.

Kohler, W. *The Mentality of Apes.* New York: Harcourt, Brace, 1927.

Kohler, W. *Gestalt Psychology.* New York: Liveright, 1929, 1947.

Latner, J. *The Gestalt Therapy Book.* New York: Julian Press, 1973.

Latner, J. "This is the speed of light: Field and systems theories in Gestalt therapy." *Gestalt Journal,* VI, no. 22, Fall 1983, 71–90.

Lewin, K. *A Dynamic Theory of Personality.* New York: McGraw-Hill, 1935.

Lewin, K. *Field Theory in Social Science.* New York: Harper, 1951(a).

Lewis, K. "Intention, will and need." in D. Rapaport (ed.), *Organization and Pathology of Thought.* New York: Columbia University Press, 1951(b).

Maslow, A. *Motivation and Personality.* New York: Harper, 1954.

Merry, U., and Brown, G. *The Neurotic Behavior of Organizations.* Cleveland: Gestalt Institute of Cleveland Press, 1987. Published and Distributed by Gardner Press.

Nevis, S.M., and Zinker, J. "How Gestalt therapy views couples, families, and the process of their psychotherapy." *Working Paper,* Center for the Study of Intimate Systems, Gestalt Institute of Cleveland, 1982.

Ovsiankina, M.R. "The resumption of interrupted activities." In J. deRivera, *Field Theory as Human Science.* New York: Gardner Press, 1976.

Papernow, P.L. "The stepfamily cycle: An experiental model of stepfamily development." *Family Relations,* July 1984.

Perls, F.S. *Ego, Hunger and Aggression.* New York: Random House, 1947, 1969.

Perls, F.S. Hefferline, R.F., and Goodman, P. *Gestalt Therapy.* New York: Dell, 1951.

Peters, T.J., and Waterman, R.H. *In Search of Excellence.* New York: Harper & Row, 1982.

Polster, E., and Polster, M. *Gestalt Therapy Integrated.* New York: Brunner/Mazel, 1973.

Pursglove, P.D. (ed.), *Recognitions in Gestalt Therapy.* New York: Funk & Wagnalls, 1968.

Riech, W. *Character Analysis.* New York: Farrar, Straus & Cudahy, 1949.

Smith, E.L. *The Growing Edge of Gestalt Therapy.* New York: Brunner/Mazel, 1976.

Wallen, R.W. "Gestalt therapy and Gestalt psychology." In Fagan and Sheperd (eds.), *Gestalt Therapy Now.* Palo Alto: Science and Behavior Books, 1970.

Wertheimer, M. *Productive Thinking.* New York: Harper, 1945.

Wysong, J., and Rosenfeld, E. "An oral history of Gestalt therapy." Highland, N.Y.: *Gestalt Journal,* 1982.

Zeigarnik, B. "On finished and unfinished tasks." In W.D. Ellis, *A Source-Book of Gestalt Psychology.* New York: Harcourt, Brace, 1938. (This research is also discussed in detail in deRivera, J., *Field Theory in Social Science,* New York: Gardner Press, 1976, pp. 111–150.)

Zinker, J. *Creative Process in Gestalt Therapy.* New York: Brunner/Mazel, 1977.

Zinker, J., and Nevis, S.M. "The Gestalt theory of couple and family interactions." *Working Paper,* Center for the Study of Intimate Systems, Gestalt Institute of Cleveland, 1981.

Zinker, J., and Nevis, S.M. *Changing Small Systems: Gestalt Theory of Couple and Family Therapy.* In Press. Cleveland: Gestalt Institute of Cleveland Press, 1988. Published and Distributed by Gardner Press.

2
The Gestalt Cycle of Experience as an Orienting Principle

We may now look at the Cycle of Experience in more detail and begin to see how it guides the practitioner of organizational consulting. Figures 1-1, 1-2 show the Cycle of Experience, both as a single, uninterrupted experience, and as the flow of continuous experiences in an ongoing process. Extensive discussions of the various phases of the Cycle have been presented elsewhere (Perls, et al., 1951; Zinker, 1977; Polster & Polster, 1973; Zinker & S. Nevis, 1981). The following discussion builds on and extends the work of these authors.

AWARENESS

Beginning with sensory arousal, the Cycle grows as awareness develops of what is going on within oneself or the surrounding environment. Awareness may be thought of as a growing consciousness or comprehension stemming from use of the senses: sight, hearing, touch, smell, and taste. Sensation provides information about what is happening and leads to the development of figures as a concern or interest is experienced. As Perls and colleagues (1951) put it:

> Sensing determines the nature of awareness, whether distant (e.g., acoustic), close (e.g., tactile), or within the skin (propri-

> oceptive). In the last term is included the sensing of one's dreams or thoughts. . . Gestalt formation always accompanies awareness.

Awareness means that something has become figural out of the many sensations or events that go on simultaneously. The aim of awareness is to enlarge and enrich potentials in the background so that what matters—what becomes figural—will be fresh, clear, and engaging. Awareness is a basic process that goes on continually (Polster & Polster, 1973):

> It is an ongoing process, readily available at all times, rather than an exclusive or sporadic illumination that can be achieved—like insight—only at special moments or under special conditions. It is always there. . . . ready to be tapped into when needed. . . . Furthermore, focusing on one's awareness keeps one absorbed in the present situation

It is important to note that awareness is not the same as introspection. True awareness is the spontaneous sensing of what arises or becomes figural, and it involves direct, immediate experience. Introspection, by contrast, is a searching, evaluative process in which parts of the experience are held up for examination—usually with the aim of studying or changing the experience. Introspection may be useful for learning about the experience, but it narrows the flow of awareness in the present moment. Carried to an extreme, introspection leads to fixation or obsession and often modifies the experience through its very act. Note the difference in allowing the full, uncensored feeling of sorrow about something hurtful said to a colleague and the act of turning quickly from this feeling to an analysis of why it was done. The former allows the experience to develop into a culminating realization, a fruition of sensation. The latter turns the experience into the act of observation and analysis. One of the significant contributions of Fritz Perls and his associates was to demonstrate that new and deep knowledge about one's behavior would derive through attending to sensation until it becomes fully heightened. Only then are the benefits of introspection valuable.

One may be aware of many different things; the whole spectrum of human experience and the basis for all knowledge and learning evolves around awareness of what is available for our comprehension. Table 2-1 lists a variety of things of which one may be aware at any given time, from direct sensation through actions, feelings, and thoughts. Note that the list incorporates memory of past events and planning for future happenings, and it encompasses the internal (awareness of self) and the external (awareness of other and of the environment in general). We all make choices within this array, choosing to attend to some things and not to attend to others. Some people have well-developed primary senses, preferring a highly "sensuous" existence, while others are more attuned to thoughts and images. Some are easily in touch with feelings, and others choose to attend to external events and are better observers of other than of self. Much of the work in self-development is devoted to improving and expanding the repertoire of awareness available to a person.

ENERGY

Out of developing awareness comes excitement or energy mobilization, which provides additional support for emergence of a clear, compelling figure. The experience with the spider web is an example of how awareness evolves from initial sensory input and is supported or limited by the amount and nature of energy mobilized to heighten and expand this awareness. The concept of energy as used here is analogous to that used in physics: energy is the ability to do work. In this instance it refers to work in developing a figure and leaving the ground momentarily behind. Lewin's notion of the tension system helps us to fix a point or place out of which this energy derives. Thus we see that energy begins to develop (we might say that there is an energy intake) from the stimulating power of awareness. Emergence of a figure in awareness leads to an energized concern. Because this concern is a springboard for action and contact, we place energy at the apex of the sine curve depicting the Cycle

Table 2-1. The Things of Which One May Be Aware (Representative List)

SENSATIONS
- The outcomes of seeing: sights
- The outcomes of hearing: sounds
- The outcomes of touching: textures, tactility
- The outcomes of gustation: tastes
- The outcomes of olfaction: smells
- The outcomes of proprioception: body tissue/kinesthetic stimulation (tendons, muscles, etc.)

INTERNAL VERBALIZATIONS AND VISUALIZATIONS
- Thinking, ruminating, internal dialogue
- Planning, wishing, hoping
- Memory, remembering past events, history
- Dreams and fantasies

FEELINGS
- Happiness, pleasure, contentment
- Elation, zest, lust, joy, confidence
- Sadness, depression, helplessness, despair
- Fear, disgust, shame, remorse
- Respect, awe, admiration, wonder, reverence
- Irritation, rage, anger, jealousy, hatred
- Vanity, self-confidence, pride
- Affection, love, warmth, empathy
- Boredom, indifference, scorn
- Tenderness, compassion, pity
- Guilt, anxiety

VALUES
- Predispositions, sets, inclinations, theories
- Judgements and attributions
- Summaries or generalizations of past experience
- Nature of boundaries, prejudices

INTERPERSONAL AND GROUP INTERACTIONS
- Participation patterns
- Communication styles
- Figural elements: content, energy, differences
- Functional activities
- Norms
- Atmosphere, climate

(Figure 2-1.) and place withdrawal at the bottom, where energy is very low and is fading. Another way to look at the Cycle is to see it as energy arousal and discharge over time.

Once developed, energy must be used. Figure 2-1 illustrates the movement from energy to action as an interesting figure be-

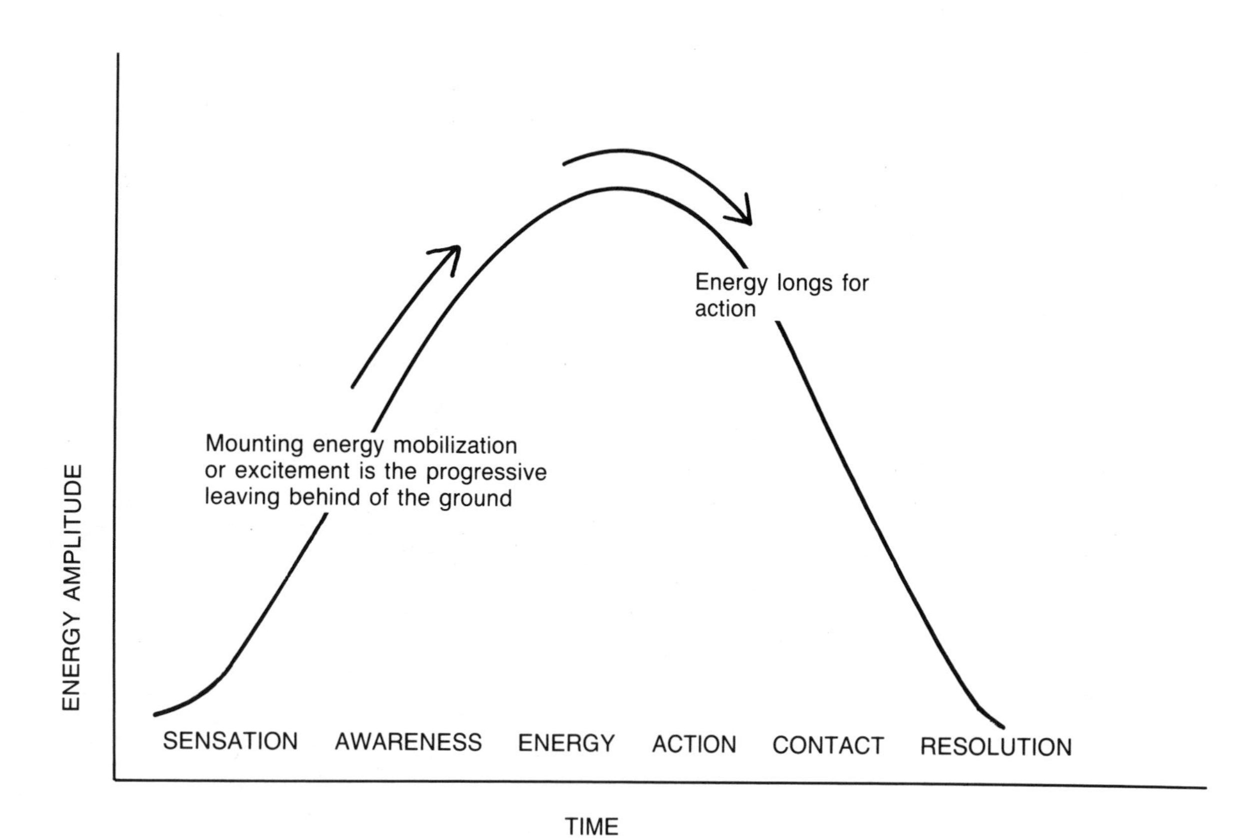

Figure 2-1. The Cycle of Experience seen as energy arousal and discharge.

comes "charged" and surrounding elements fade into the background.

ACTION AND CONTACT

Thus far the flow describes a change in the perception of self and/or the surrounding world, and a mounting interest in attending to it. Uninterrupted flow then leads into an action step in which motoric behavior is added to the perceptual. This is the task of tying together the aroused energy with the behavioral skills, knowledge, or competence of the individual in a way that some appropriate action takes place. The integration of sensory awareness and motor behavior is called *contact*, and it involves more than just reaching out for or stretching toward a complete experience. Contact involves an aggressive response to a figure of interest, a form of active participation in which the figure is literally transformed through work to comprehend and assimilate it. In *Ego, Hunger, and Aggression* (1947, 1969), Fritz Perls presents insights into the way the organism assimilates things from the environment. Using constructs such as "mental food," "oral aggression," and "dental inhibition," he shows the importance of physical and mental destruction of things engaged by the person if true assimilation is to occur. One must "take something apart," if one is to know it fully. By this Perls did not mean that the object or person is literally destroyed, but that the perceiver changes his or her own perceptual and cognitive awareness by internally "chewing" on the object. Using eating as an analogous process, he illustrates the important difference between swallowing without chewing and the much richer experience of knowing that one has eaten by really chewing on food. He aptly provides a correction to the Freudian notion of introjection, which he views as a straight preservation of the structure of the introjected item—unaware swallowing versus aware chewing. With the phases of food consumption as a model, he studied the process by which the world in general is mentally absorbed by people. In his scheme true contact cannot occur without such a "working-through" process. He defines the resistances of introjection, projection, retroflection, and confluence as failures in doing the work necessary to heighten awareness and move toward contact. Thus contact is that phase of the Cycle of Experience in which a fully developed experience emerges from working with a figure of great interest. We acknowledge contact, for example, when we say: "I finally got through to him," "I was moved by what you said," or "I learned something in that discussion."

Contact occurs at the boundary of self and other. This is another way of saying that all figures, no matter how much time and energy are available for their formation, have an ending point or boundary that defines them and distinguishes them from the background. Through psychic work one can change this point—either opening or decreasing the boundary perimeter—or one can rest comfortably with what *is* at any moment. In the example of the spider web, contact was defined at a visual boundary. I did study it visually in some detail, but within very narrow, closed auditory, olfactory, and gustatory boundaries. Rich figures were not developed in the latter modalities. In fact, I only became aware of how closed my boundaries were regarding use of these sensory modalities with the web when I started to describe my experience. As contact is an essential aspect of learning and change, I would need to deal with or face these boundaries to see whether I was willing to change them in any way. I can live well without touching or tasting a spider web as long as I am content with a certain level of knowledge, but I cannot carry my learning further without confronting the boundary I have created.

In terms of the need-fulfillment nature of Gestalt therapy, contact is the point at which there is attainment of need satisfaction, with satisfaction being defined as the full, heightened experience as to how, where, and in what way the need is met. There is no assumption in this perspective that an automatic, full satisfaction of need as initially experienced will take place. Contact is defined as knowing what is possible, not achieving what is desired. For example, I may be hungry but learn that the stores are closed and that I have only a small amount of not-very-appealing food available to eat at that moment. Likewise, I may desire a close relationship with another manager, but I learn through attempts to get closer that the other wants a more formal, distant relationship. Thus it is not correct to say: "I could not reach her," and assume that no contact was made. On the contrary, what is correct to say is that a particular contact was achieved and that this contact is described by the phenomenologically different boundary experiences of the two people involved. This is not a mere play on words; it is an acknowledgment that to make contact of any kind is to learn something about the present state of affairs. Contact does not mean achieving a goal or having a "peak" experience. Contact is the uniting of a desired goal with the possible.

RESOLUTION AND CLOSURE

From contact, which we see as learning relative to what is possible in the individual–environment interaction, comes resolution and closure. This means culminating the action by turning to comprehension or knowledge of what has been learned, and to assimilation of the experience. Contact is the experience from which meaning is extracted; resolution is the act of extracting meaning and recognizing that closure has occurred, and that the situation is finished or complete. Once meaning is extracted, we can say that learning has occurerd. After this, withdrawal of attention from the figure takes place—the figure has been destroyed—and a gradual subsiding of energy and interest takes place. There has been a cessation of work and a Cycle has been completed. This makes possible readiness for new awareness to develop. What has been learned becomes part of the ground and is available for later use.

GESTALT INTERACTIVE CYCLE

Up to this point, the Cycle has been discussed in terms of one person, or for a unified, singular process of a group of two or more. However, the reality of organizational systems of any kind is that they are made up of many cycles. Each member of the system lives in his or her own life-space at any given time. The awareness of each member will be unique, depending upon many factors. What each will be able to attend to will vary, and what each will allow to come into awareness will be different. The energy available for dealing with any issue or task will also vary, sometimes greatly. The test of organizational effectiveness, or leadership ability, is to bring this kaleidescope of awareness-energy patterns into sharp focus so that good decisions can be made and implemented. Otherwise dysfunctional behavior prevails. In terms of need identification and satisfaction: how does a system of more than one person regulate, modulate, or integrate the different needs or tension systems of its members?

To deal with this question, we conceptualize organization as analogous to a living organism, and we hypothesize that the Cycle of Experience and the figure-ground paradigm holds at this larger system level as it does for the individual. From this perspective it then becomes possible to adapt the Cycle as an orienting principle for work with organizational units. We simply assume that there are coexisting Cycles and that an organization–environment relationship requires an adaptation process similar to an individual adaptation process. A system of two or more people requires a means of tuning into its needs and of mobilizing energy just as an individual does. For healthy functioning, survival, and growth, an organization requires an effective way of making good contact across the innumerable boundaries that make up subsystems. Each time a system is enlarged in size or scope of tasks, the situational dynamics are compounded in complexity, but the general requirements for adaptation or growth appear to be no different than for individuals. For good system functioning, the processes of awareness, energy mobilization, and contact need to operate at a high level. Breakdowns at any point, as an interruption in the flow of the cycle, can lead to impairment of system effectiveness in carrying out its major tasks.

To capture the situation in family systems of two or more people, Zinker and S. Nevis (1981) have conceptualized the "Gestalt Interactive Cycle." The phases of the Cycle of Experience remain the same as for individuals, but attention is now focused on the Cycle for each individual and the interactions among the members of the system. The focus here is not only directed toward self-awareness but, equally important, toward attending to and becoming more interested in noticing, hearing from, and responding to others. There is a premium on digging into oneself so as to be fully in touch and as clear as possible in articulating self-awareness, but an equally important effort is required for listening to and understanding others. It is this interplay of expressed awareness among the people involved that is critical for the stimulation of energy in the group.

The concept of the Gestalt Interactive Cycle is designed to assist in understanding how an organizational unit of any size integrates the different awareness, energy, and contact patterns into effective system functioning. Figure 2-2 indicates how this might work in an ideal setting. In this example, individuals A, B, C, and D have different starting points and varying rates and scopes of awareness development. The shaded area on the left side of the Cycle represents the domain of all awareness generated by these four people around the issue at hand. Person A becomes interested in the issue earlier than do the others, but shows a slower rate of acceleration in energy than do B or C, whose awareness develops slightly later but intensifies more rapidly. The important thing is that, as they interact, the individual Cycles meet at the apex: energy emerging from their awareness leads to a new figure—a group or collective creation. To achieve this fresh figure requires a great deal of sharing among the people involved and a lot of solicitation and interest in what the others are thinking and feeling about the subject at hand. The aim in this phase is to achieve the fullest, widest band of awareness possible. If this phase is rushed or curtailed, there is diminished opportunity to get at the relevant data needed to form a new group figure. However, done well and unhurried, the interaction results in a joining together around a fresh figure of interest to all. This leads to related, supportive actions that may be different for the four people involved, but are unified by the common figure. Thus there may be varying degrees of intensity in the contacts among the people, and the nature of the meaning of the experience may be different for each, but their behavior is synergistic. The narrower band on the right slope of the

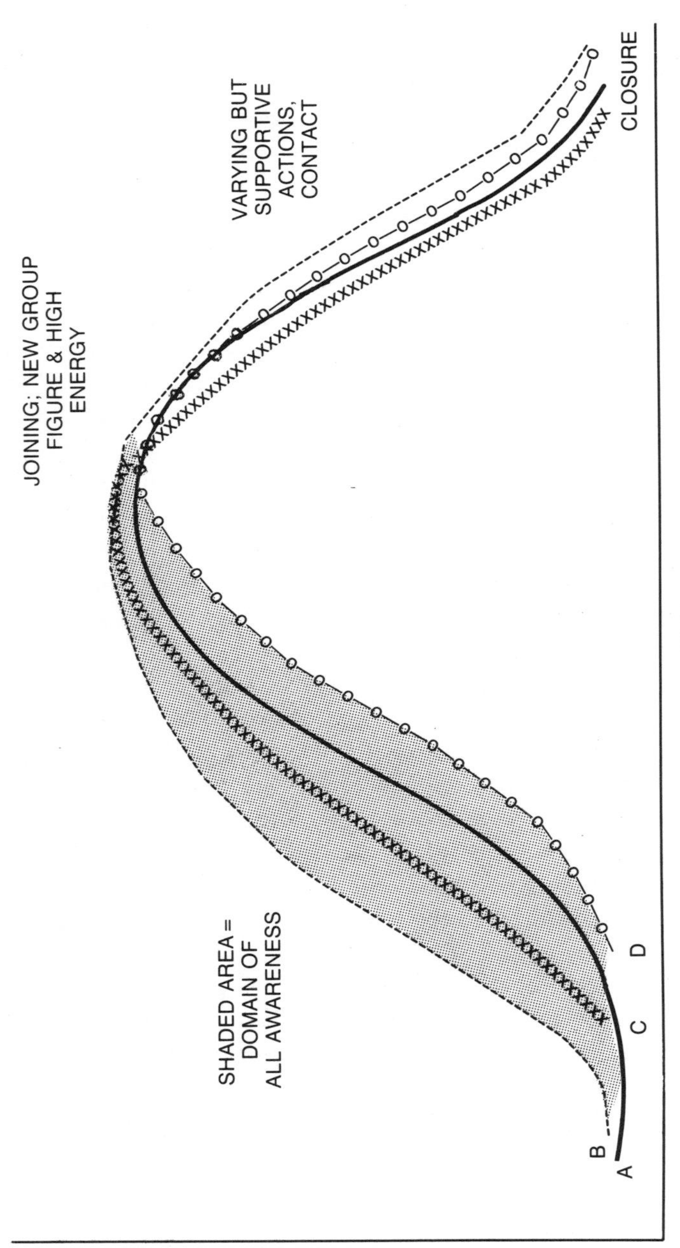

PERSON A = ————

PERSON B = – – – – –

PERSON C = xxxxxxxxxxxxx

PERSON D = —o—o—o—o

Figure 2-2. Gestalt Interactive Cycle: an ideal situation.

Cycle shows that there are differences among the people but, since there was a joining around a new group figure, the spread of the differences is less than in the awareness phase. This is what is meant by integration of individual attitudes, needs, styles, and so on into effective system functioning. The test of this integration does not demand that all be at the same place, or that unanimity exists. The test is that there is again a coming together at the point of closure: the four people know and accept that a "best possible" unit of work has been completed, one that contributes to the well-being of the unit.

In order to grasp the value of the interactive Cycle, we can look at some examples in which a full or easy coming together does not occur. Figure 2-3 derived from Zinker and S. Nevis' (1981) work with families, illustrates this situation. In this figure we have an example of four people—father, mother, sister, and brother—and we see that at this moment they are not at the same place with regard to the family task or problem depicted by this pattern of Cycles. If we assume that the individual members of a family have different styles and skills of awareness, it is easy to see the existence of the pattern given. Indeed, this is the usual pattern in all but the most confluent systems. In addition, it is likely that in a family system the individual members will have different "rhythms" for contact; for instance, some will want more intense interactions than others, and some will want to be alone when others want partial or total family contact. Thus when it comes to dealing with a given issue, the energy of some family members will lag behind that of others. Furthermore, whether or not something is seen as a problem will vary among the members. These variations hold for single aspects of daily living as well as for serious problems. As an illustration, you might recall a discussion in your own family about what to do on a Sunday afternoon or on a vacation. To achieve a good decision in such a discussion requires identification of and sharing of such things as each person's awareness, needs, and energy so that a truly systemwide Cycle emerges.

Figure 2-3 depicts an instance in which the father, mother, and sister are reasonably close in awareness and energy at this moment of interaction, but the brother is at another place. Or-

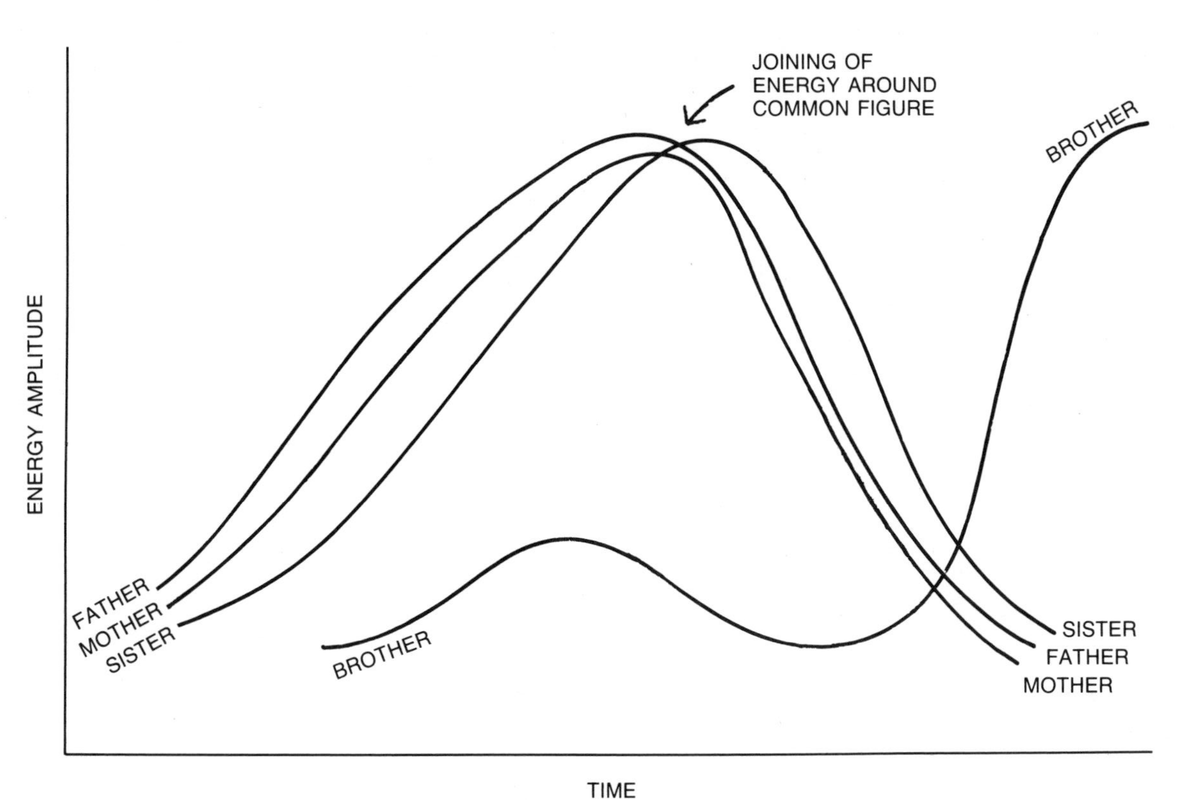

Figure 2-3. Gestalt Interactive Cycle as applied in a family system.

dinarily there is a tendency to see the brother as "resisting" what the others want to do. I prefer to look at this situation as an instance of *multidirected energy*, to be respectful of the fact that the brother's Cycle has an integrity of its own, and that the family system can be seen as being made up of different but equally valid needs and wants. This way of viewing what is normally called "resistance" is elaborated in detail in Chapter 8.

The phases of the four Cycles in Figure 2-3 show that the father, mother, and sister are close together in awareness, energy mobilization, contact, and resolution. The brother does not join with them, even though he makes a slight movement toward their figure. His energy dies down well before it can join with the energy of the others, and the brother remains more interested in his awareness. This leads to development of his own energy at a time when the others remain close together around their joined energy. Without knowing more about this family and its decision-making practices, we cannot tell whether this is an unhappy state of affairs; it often happens that one member of a family prefers to do something different from the others. However, if it is essential for some purpose that all members join together in awareness about and energy to deal with an issue, this cannot be a "best possible" resolution. At any rate, it is the interaction among the family members that allows for movement from initially variant Cycles to an outcome in which the members become an integrated unit or decide to go separate ways.

Figures 2-4, 2-5, and 2-6 show other patterns in a system of four people. In all of these examples, we start with the initial awareness of the individual members as they interact with each other. These Interactive Cycles depict three different situations that occur frequently in organizational life.

Figure 2-4 illustrates an instance in which variations in the amount and depth of effort devoted to the awareness phase leads to action that appears to be supported by high energy but is not. Person A becomes aware of the issue earlier than the others, but does not develop a powerful figure and significant energy until just before group action occurs. The issue enters into Person B's awareness a bit later than it does for Person A, but Person B has a rich, relatively unhurried awareness phase that leads to a high level of energy. Persons C and D become aware of the issue even

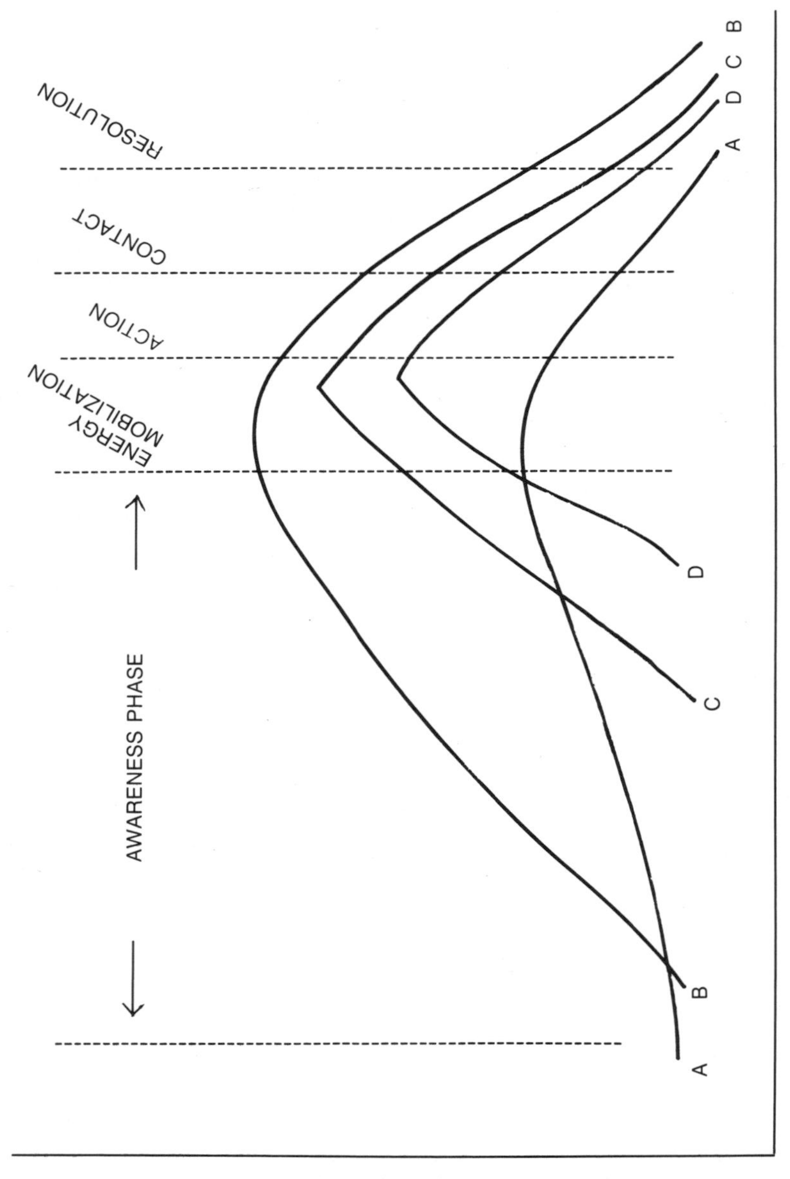

Figure 2-4. Gestalt Interactive Cycle showing weak joining around a group figure.

later than Person B, and go through very brief awareness periods; they mobilize energy that is greater than that of Person A, but not as strong as that of Person B. The combined energy leads to the action phase of this interaction, and a decision is made. However, if we look at the contact phase, we see that these people are not synchronized as to a common understanding of the issue and what has been decided. We can say that the members of the group are in different places as to their contact with (their knowledge of) the problem and where each stands with regard to it. An example of this in organizational life is when some members of a management group think that a problem has been sufficiently studied and start a course of action only to find out later that a consensus did not exist. Though the family example of Figure 2-3 shows varying awareness and energy patterns among the individuals, there is a point at which three of them come together around a common problem definition and can understand where each is with respect to this issue. In Figure 2-4 we see that the four people do not come together about contact or resolution. This decision is not likely to result in effective implementation by the group.

Figure 2-5 is an illustration of long awareness and relatively flat energy phases for all four members of the group. An example of this can be seen in groups that are prone to obsess and agonize a great deal over issues, and for whom polite behavior is a strong norm. The result is that bland rather than powerful actions will ensue as the group has difficulty in achieving a high level of energy, and is unable to move into a risk-taking or entrepreneurial mode.

Another pattern is presented in Figure 2-6. This example may be best described as one in which all do "their own thing." Each person in this group may be concerned with the same problem but each is at a very different place as to awareness, energy, and so forth. If uncoordinated effort is sufficient to deal with the problem, this state of affairs is fine. On the other hand, if highly integrated effort is required, this group will be very ineffective as a collective entity.

If the number of people in a work unit or organizational system increases, such as in an eight- or ten-person managerial group, the picture of an Interactive Cycle becomes even more

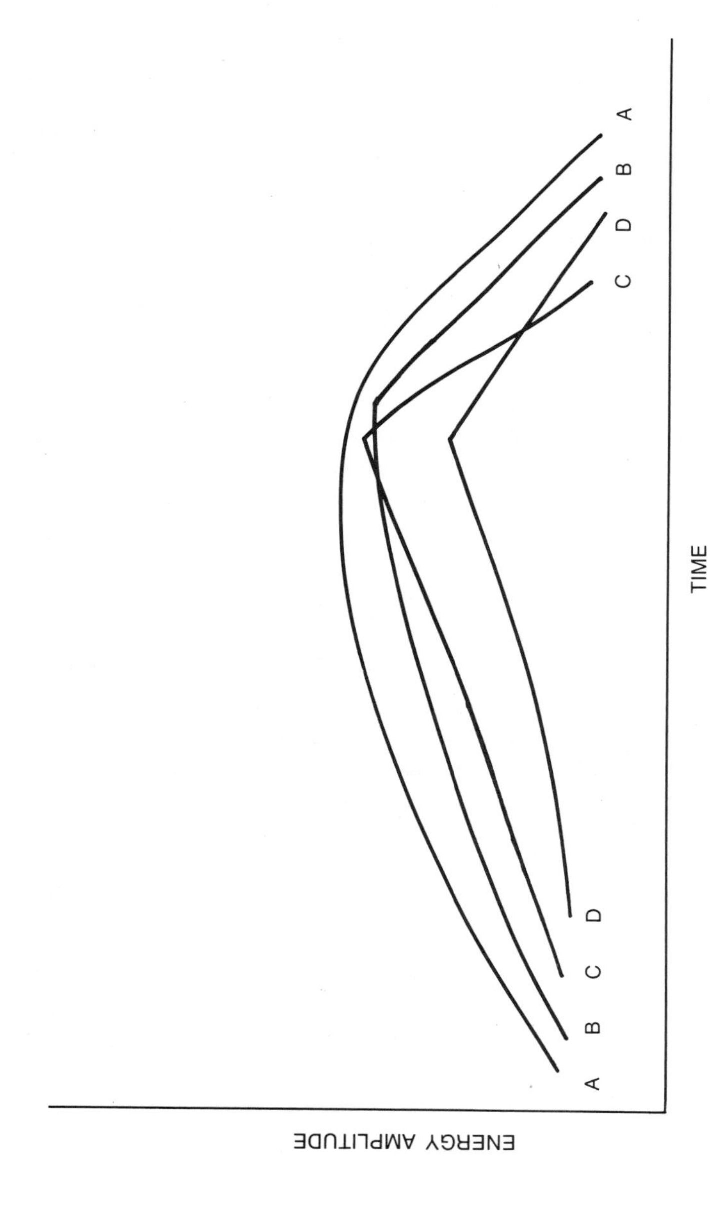

Figure 2-5. Gestalt Interactive Cycle showing flat energy pattern.

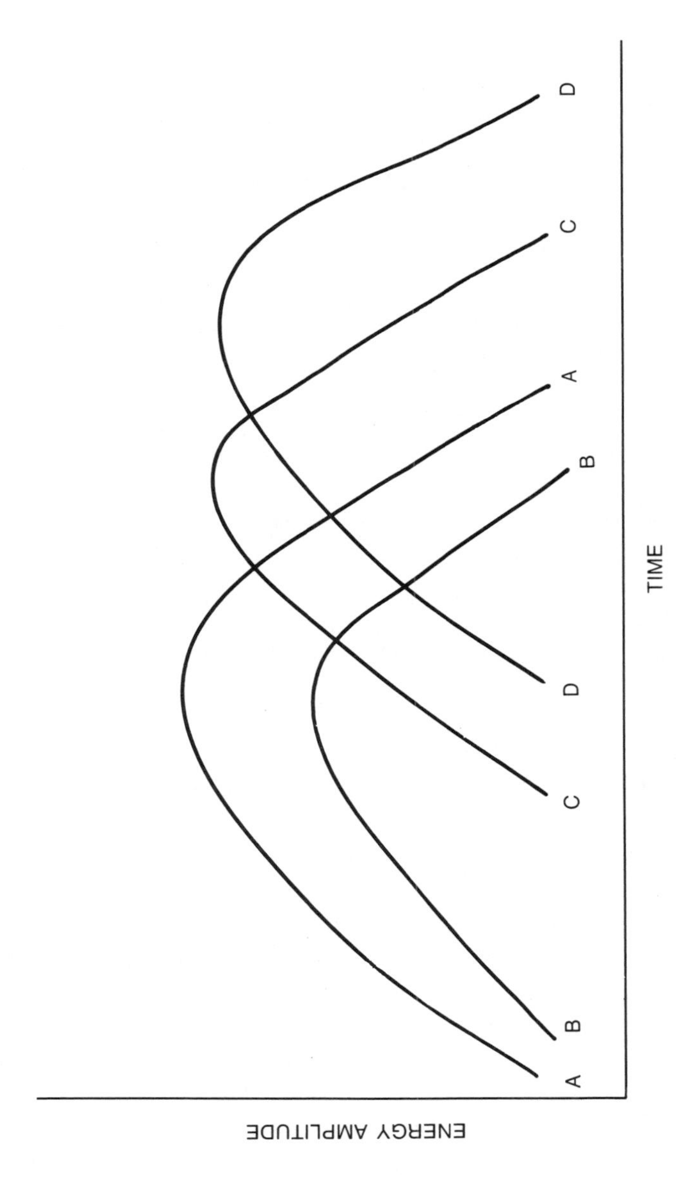

Figure 2-6. Gestalt Interactive Cycle showing an uncoordinated group.

complicated than in the above examples. Failure to appreciate this reality and to deal with it effectively is an important reason why organizations do not function at optimal levels of effectiveness. As a result we see poor techniques for sharing and obtaining information, let alone knowing how to achieve consensus (common figure) when divergent views are on the table. Actions are often based on skimpy awareness, or in settings where the energy of one or two people pulls along a reluctant majority. The existence of these inefficiencies defines the general objectives of the Gestalt-oriented organization consultant:

1. To help the client system understand the Interactive Cycle of Experience and to learn to function better in carrying out the process of awareness, contact, etc.
2. To help each member of the system to articulate his or her awareness and encourage and notice the awareness of others, so that each member knows what the other is thinking and feeling with regard to the issue at hand; to help lay bare and heighten the existing figures so that a new group figure can emerge and be acted upon.
3. To behave personally in such a way as to model the processes of the Cycle; to become a finely honed instrument for the observation of self and other; to provide an active presence that stimulates the learning of the client system.

APPLICATION TO ORGANIZATIONAL CONSULTING

From the above it should be apparent that the present approach falls within the domain of process consultation and is directed toward a microlevel of analysis. In the following chapter, this position and the tasks of the consultant are expanded and compared with other well-known approaches to process consultation. For the reader who may not be an experienced process consultant, one way to grasp the applicability of the Interactive Cycle as an orienting principle is to see it as a way of helping people look at their behavior while trying to solve a problem or make a decision. We can compare the phases of the Cycle with stages in managerial decision making. Table 2-2 presents this relationship and begins to define those behaviors

Table 2-2. The Relationship of Phases in the Gestalt Cycle of Experience to Stages of Managerial Decision Making*

Cycle Phase	*Corresponding Managerial Decision-Making Behavior*
Awareness	Data generation Seeking of information Sharing of information Reviewing performance history Environmental scanning
Energy/action	Any attempt to mobilize energy and interest in ideas or proposals Supporting ideas presented by others Joining with what is important to others Any attempt to identify differences and conflicts or competing interests Supporting own position Seeking maximum participation
Contact	Joining in a common objective Common recognition of problem definition Indications of understanding, not necessarily agreement Choosing a course of future action that is possible
Resolution/closure	Testing; checking for common understanding Reviewing what has occurred Acknowledgment of what was accomplished and what remains to be done Identifying the meaning of the discussion Generalizing from what has been learned Beginning to develop implementation and action plans
Withdrawal	Pausing to let things "sink in" Reducing energy and interest in the issue Turning to other tasks or problems Ending the meeting

*See Zinker and S. Nevis (1981) for a similar version applied to family decision-making processes.

of interest to the consultant. The importance of the relationship shown is that it clarifies the work of the consultant and offers a guideline for effective intervention and teaching. Using the Cycle as orientation, the consultant acts as an instrument that observes and monitors the decision-making process of the client system to see that each phase is carried out well, and that there is an appreciation for the unity of an entire Cycle. Moreover, the consultant bases intervention on what is missing in the system and what is needed to improve the process.

At first look, the phases of the Cycle may appear to correspond roughly to stages of organizational consulting. Certainly the entry and assessment stages of consultation place a heavy emphasis on awareness development. During these stages the consultant searches for figural concerns, and tries to see what potentials exist for energy mobilization around those that are important. Most educational interventions serve a similar consciousness-raising function. Likewise, we see that third-party interventions, confrontation meetings, and other conflict resolution methods are designed to stretch or enlarge contact boundaries or to build on fragile contacts. However, it would be a mistake to see the Cycle in such a limited or fragmented relationship to the consulting process. The Cycle of Experience defines a basic process of awareness that the consultant deals with in self and other while carrying out the work at each stage of consultation.

Awareness is the starting point from which all the work proceeds. The data derived from awareness guide each stage of the consultation process: awareness enables the consultant to determine what an organization is about and how it functions; it enables the consultant to decide if a good, mutually rewarding relationship with the client is possible; it leads to decisions about appropriate interventions; and it lets the consultant know how the work is going and what is preventing system growth or effectiveness. In Nadler's (1977) book on the use of survey-feedback data in organization development, he recognizes this in discussing how data are used by the consultant at each stage of the consultation process. Table 2-3 provides a summary of his perspective that can be related to the present one by substituting the word "awareness" for "data."

A PHENOMENOLOGICAL CONCEPTION OF DATA

The importance of broad awareness that leads to effective energy mobilization and action will be readily appreciated by

Table 2-3. Uses of Data in Different Stages of Organization Development*

Stages of Organization Development (from Kolb & Frohman, 1970)	*Typical Uses of Data*
Scouting/entry	*Orientation:* Data used to get a feel for the client organization's basic characteristics and to find out if there is a basis for a relationship.
Diagnosis	*Diagnosis:* Data used to develop a comprehensive and in-depth picture of the client's system: its operations, its employees' attitudes, its strong points, and its major problems and their causes.
Planning	*Planning interventions:* Data used to determine what interventions are appropriate, where they should be applied, and how they should be implemented.
Action	*Motivating change:* Data used to motivate individuals or groups to unfreeze or begin changing and to initiate the change process.
Evaluation/termination	*Monitoring and assessing interventions:* Data used to track the progress of interventions as they are implemented and to assess the costs and benefits of interventions after they are completed.

*David A. Nadler, FEEDBACK AND ORGANIZATION DEVELOPMENT, © 1977, Addison-Wesley Publishing Company, Inc., Reading, Massachusetts. Pg. 17, Fig. 1.2. Reprinted with permission.

those who do action research and survey feedback interventions. These methods rely on the principle of "data as an energizing force," and are based on assumptions similar to those that underlie the figure-ground model of the Cycle of Experience. The Gestalt conception, however, has two elements that make it a potent addition to data-based intervention methods. First, stemming from a phenomenological perspective, awareness in the Gestalt model is a broader concept than are usual definitions of data or information. The latter connote logical, hard facts—events that are relatively easy to summarize or quantify, and that imply linear thinking or an "objective reality." Most managers and many consultants equate data with externally observable facts. This propensity has driven the field of organization development toward an overly rational perspective. However, as we see in Table 2-1 the objects of awareness include images, fantasies, dreams, and feelings, those events that we tend to consider subjective or irrational. These are real, powerful determinants of behavior—even if they may be idiosyncratic aspects of behavior.

A second contribution derives from the Interactive Cycle. This concept tells us that what data are, and how people will respond to data, may vary considerably among individuals in the same group or work unit. This approach takes as a given the notion that variety exists as to awareness and energy levels in any situation involving two or more people. The work of the consultant is to deal with these differential effects as though they were all "hard facts" and important statements of reality. This allows for every individual's inner experience to be weighted equally in the quest for a collective figure that can be acted upon by the group.

COMPLETION OF UNITS OF WORK

The concept of the Cycle of Experience accepts as a premise the importance of data—or awareness in the Gestalt framework—but goes further in that it relates awareness to the development of actions that lead to culminating learning experiences. It is a model of behavior that conceptualizes what might be called "a unit of work." The value of seeing experience as a unit of work is that consultants can orient themselves to view each interaction with client systems in terms of a beginning and an ending. The consultant who uses the Cycle as an orienting principle sees each and every session with a client as requiring a completed unit of work. He or she is constantly observant of how each phase develops, and of what needs to be done in each phase in order for a useful experience to take place. Whether engaged in individual counseling, two-person planning, or group meeting, the objective is to ensure that all phases of the Cycle have been dealt with adequately. Interventions follow from the consultant's sense of what will enhance an orderly, appropriate flow through the process. An important aspect of this is that the client system knows and accepts at the end of the intervention that a unit of work was accomplished. A Cycle has been completed in some way: there is a clear idea of what has been done, of what has not been done, and/or of what the system is not ready to deal with at that time. Thus I work to make sure that the members of the system can make some statements at the end of the session that summarize the experience and signify the meaning of the experience for the life of the system. This is true for a one-hour interaction, a three-day retreat, or an extended assignment.

Though it is not expected that a consultant will orient around the Cycle in a blind, mechanical manner, failure to see that a phase has been dealt with adequately before going on to the next phase can lead to disastrous results. This was made clear to me about 20 years ago when I was working with a large accounting firm. My partners and I were engaged in an ongoing management development and organization development effort for a fast-growing organization. Preparatory to launching team-building efforts in those regions in which a managing partner would request it, we designed and conducted a three-day session as part of the annual meeting of all the managing partners—about 50 people. For the managing partners' meeting, the major intervention was to share questionnaire data obtained from a 25 percent sample of the firm's employees and managers, and from the 50 partners in attendance at that meeting. The objective was to allow the partners at the meeting to compare their picture of organizational concerns and personal needs of the professional staff with those obtained from the staff itself. Only three or four of these managing partners had been involved with us in the planning of the meeting and the design of the survey. In presenting the findings, we aroused a great deal of negative reaction from the partners. We were told that the data were inaccurate, and that we had presented useless, possibly false, information. Information certainly energized the recipients of it, but the result was disbelief and hostility toward the data, our method of obtaining the data, and us.

In analyzing this situation, it became clear that the data obtained had enhanced our awareness considerably. What was figural for us, and the four partners who worked with us in the design of the intervention, was clear and sharp to the extent that our data made possible. However, we had not done enough to enhance our awareness of the ability of the full group of partners to take in the data, or of their readiness to enter into open discussion of the data. If we had talked to more partners initially, perhaps sending them the survey results for private review prior to the meeting, we might have begun to heighten their awareness in a safer setting, or at least obtained their negative reactions beforehand. We might have interviewed more partners at the start to see if they were ready for this kind of intervention, but we proceeded on skimpy, limited awareness and moved into an attempt to mobilize energy and action with insufficient support in the client system. In other words, we moved the partners into what was an experimental situation without having their consent for the experiment, or a good picture of their willingness to deal with this group experiment. We might have been pleased with the reaction we did obtain, for it told us much about our client system, but we generated so much negativism that only two regions were interested enough to go ahead with team building. Poor process at the awareness level seriously hurt any efforts to proceed to the next phase of the Cycle. We learned that we had to back up considerably in our work with this organization, finding less threatening means of raising awareness before moving into high-contact confrontation sessions. It became clear that a longer, more varied period of awareness development is necessary when working with a large group or a complex organizational unit.

This example may be pictured in terms of the Interactive Cycle of Experience. Based on a joining by a subset of members of the system with the consultants, an action step was implemented. But the awareness of most of the members was directed elsewhere, and these people were not ready to make contact with the data in the same way that the subset was prepared to do.

REFERENCES

Nadler, D.A. *Feedback and Organization Development: Using Data-Based Methods.* Reading, Mass.: Addison-Wesley, 1977.

Perls, F.S. *Ego, Hunger, and Aggression.* New York: Random House, 1947, 1969.

Perls, F.S., Hefferline, R.F., and Goodman, P. *Gestalt Therapy.* New York: Dell, 1951.

Polster, E., and Polster, M. *Gestalt Therapy Integrated.* New York: Brunner/Mazel, 1973.

Zinker, J. *Creative Process in Gestalt Therapy.* New York: Brunner/Mazel, 1977.

Zinker, J., and Nevis, S.M. "The Gestalt theory of couple and family interactions." *Working Paper,* Center for the Study of Intimate Systems, Gestalt Institute of Cleveland, 1981.

3
A Gestalt Model of Organizational Intervention

THE ACT OF INTERVENTION

All acts of organizational consulting can be considered interventions. While the use of the term "intervention" is awkward and implies a grandeur that is not always present in consulting work, intervention conveys what is involved in trying to help an organization: intervention means *to enter into* an ongoing system for the purpose of helping it in some way. The consultant may do this in a manner that allows the work of the organization to go on more or less without interruption, but the very nature of coming between or among the individuals, groups, objects, or structures of an organization changes the situation in a fundamental way. Acts of intervention—the making of observations, the introduction of learning experiences and other supportive procedures—are designed or intended to affect the ongoing social process. Holding aside, for the moment, the question of whether the consultant's objective is to ensure that change takes place, intervenors are expected to behave in a way that makes a contribution to the improved functioning of the client system. Presumably the very presence of the consultant serves to heighten awareness about some aspect of the system.

In daily conversation, I use the word "consulting" more than the word "intervening," but I stress the latter when teaching students. I do this to counteract a lack of awareness on the part of many consultants, especially trainees and relatively inexperienced practitioners, of the potential awesomeness of the undertaking. To put it in perspective, I tell students that the best way to appreciate this is to imagine that their family has just been diagnosed as having problems, and that it has been recommended that a helper live with the family for several months in order to be of assistance to them. One's feelings about family intervention are much more complex and intense than those related to the work situation. The gasps and nervous laughter of the students in response to this comment underscore the significance of what is at issue in any intervention.

It is also important to realize that, by definition, an intervenor is different in some important aspect from the members of the client organization. This difference is a complex issue that has important implications both with respect to the restrictions upon what an intervenor can accomplish and to the opportunities that such difference makes possible. To a degree, the attractiveness of a given consultant lies in the perceived skills and orientation of that consultant. These competencies are not seen as necessary by a potential client if they merely repeat or reflect skills and attitudes that exist in the organization. (The possible exception might be the direct purchase of "extra hands" to fill out a work team to finish a specific task that is well-defined.) On the other hand, if the values and the approaches for which the consultant is known are far removed from the acceptable range of possibilities in the client culture, that client is not likely to select the consultant or will develop a great deal of resistance to utilizing the consultant in an optimal way. If acceptable intervenors in a given system fall somewhere between these extremes, we may assume a constant push–pull dynamic in which forces are exerted to keep the intervenor "like us," as well as encouraging what is different. The artful use of the tension created by sameness and difference issues can work to the consultant's advantage, or it can be a major source of difficulty and potential consultant failure if not managed well. To make the most of this tension, the effective consultant remains constantly aware of it and does not try to eliminate or brush it aside.

It follows, then, that any act of intervention may be seen as an act of arrogance or presumption on the part of the intervenor.

Aside from the assumption that the consultant is capable of helping by virtue of experience and reputation, there is the assumption that the client cannot see clearly or act wisely enough to solve a particular problem without the help of an outsider. Once there is even small recognition that the consultant has wisdom or perception related to distance and objectivity, it immediately elevates him or her above the client in some way. While a client system may admire the consultant's differences, it is likely to be very ambivalent about the hints of superiority that come with such elevation. Given this, and the fact that the intervenor comes into an ongoing social system that has a history and a pattern of norms and values, to take a consulting assignment means that one is willing to accept the challenge and the burdens that come with acts of presumption. How one achieves an integration of authority and humility will be critical to the success or failure of the relationship.

Intervention as Boundary Changing

A related consideration in understanding the act of intervention is that it involves assertive moves that affect the boundaries between the system and its environment. Thus an act of intervention may be performed by a person who is clearly outside the normal boundary of the intervened system, and in some way becomes attached to it. The classic example of this is the hiring of a consulting firm in order to obtain the services of "external consultants." Figure 3-1 shows the boundary situation in this instance.

Another very common situation is one in which an individual with a special relationship, or a role attached to the system or a subsystem of the client organization, is asked to do a particular piece of work. This is the model for corporate staff people who have "dotted-line" responsibilities for operations, and it embraces the relatively new role of internal consultant. This model also relates to an individual who is temporarily assigned to a special task force in order to bring about some change. Figure 3-2 defines this boundary relationship.

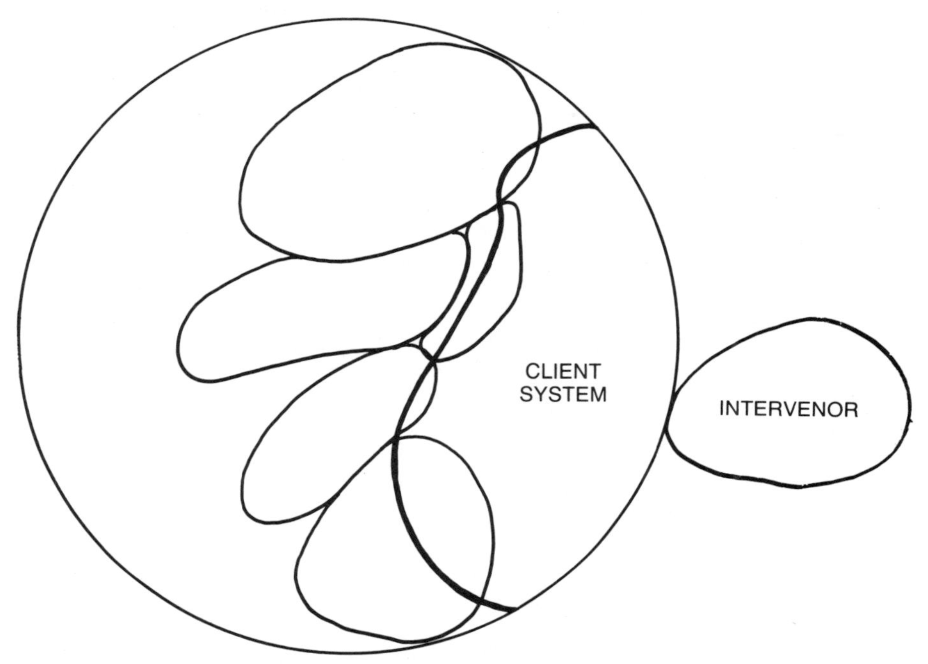

Figure 3-1. Intervenor outside the normal boundary of the client system.

Finally included under the category of "acts of intervention" are those instances where either the leader or a member of a work group undertakes a plan or program to bring about change. In these cases the intervenor is clearly inside the normal boundary of the system but temporarily *elevates* himself or herself to a special role. While this may seem to be normal job-related behavior, it is useful to label it as intervention. This individual, at the moment of elevation, acts with the same kind of arrogance or presumption to be found in those intervenors not normally considered to be full members of the work system. This relationship is depicted in Figure 3-3.

It will be seen that this perspective encompasses the question of boundaries in general and issues concerning consultant marginality. In Chapter 9 there is a more detailed discussion of marginality and working at the boundary. For now it is important to recognize that the act of consulting is one of crossing over or changing a social system boundary. To consult or to intervene

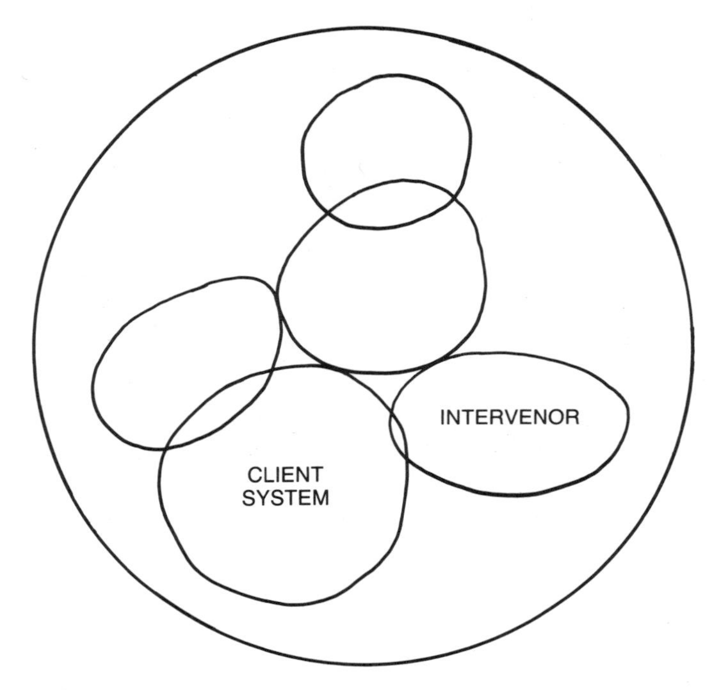

Figure 3-2. Intervenor in a special role within the client boundary.

places one in the position of being a disturber of boundaries.

The boundary between client system and consultant is only one boundary that may be disturbed as the client and consultant attempt to establish good contact. If we think of a system as being made up of many subsystems, (such as a production or service system, reward systems, policies and procedures, relationships with other organization units), we can visualize boundaries around and between each of these. Any intervention that serves to heighten awareness about such subsystems is likely to focus attention on these boundaries. The task of enhancing client awareness requires examination of the ways in which current structures and processes are accepted and owned by the client system, and of how it is that alternatives are not known or accepted. The consultant who is too zealous in this regard may generate opposition; one who is not compelling enough may be ignored. At any rate, no learning can occur for the client with-

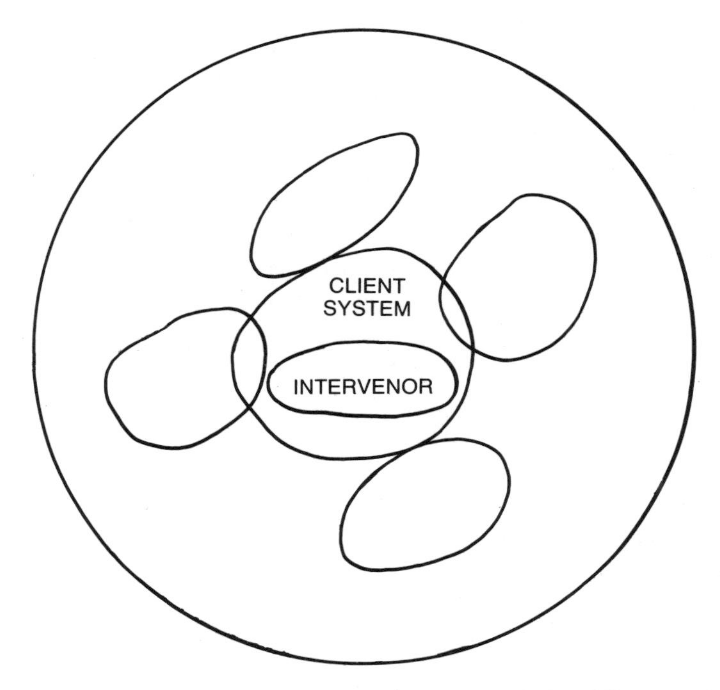

Figure 3-3. Intervenor who is a member of the client system.

out some attempt by the consultant to have the client take a fresh look at the boundaries.

GESTALT MODEL FOR INTERVENTION

With the definitions of intervention and the Cycle of Experience as background, it is possible to state the important aspects of a Gestalt perspective for organization consulting. Two major aims guide this perspective.

1. The role of the consultant is to *teach the client system* those skills necessary for understanding the Cycle of Experience and for functioning better in carrying out the processes of awareness, contact, etc.
2. In the process of helping the client system to improve its functioning, the consultant is to *provide a presence* that is otherwise lacking.

The first goal is similar to that of all consultation—to help the client function more effectively. What makes this approach different is the use of the Cycle of Experience, with its emphasis on phases of energy development and action deriving out of awareness. The notion of complete units of work is also given prominence in this framework. The Cycle has been discussed at length, and later sections of this book will deal with how it is applied by the consultant. At this point some words about providing a presence—the second objective—will be useful.

INTERVENTION AS PROVIDING A PRESENCE

This principle relates mainly to who the consultant is, and to what the consultant's general orientation and outlook are with regard to the solution of organization problems. In the Gestalt approach, the fullest use of presence is critical. The consultant is not only to stand for and express certain values, attitudes, and skills, but to use these in a way to stimulate, and perhaps *evoke* from the client, action necessary for movement on its problems. This means that the consultant is generally more open and revealing about his or her thoughts and feelings than might be true in other forms of process consultation. The aim is to take advantage of the issues of difference, marginality, and attraction by the client so as to use oneself in the most powerful way possible. Thus the Gestalt-oriented organization consultant primarily focuses on *interaction with the client* as the means through which movement toward improved organizational functioning will occur. Specifically, the consultant models a way of approaching problems and, through interest in the attractiveness of this way of being, hopes to mobilize the energy of the client system.

The following case illustrates how presence acts in the service of the consulting relationship. This example is selected to show the impact of powerful interaction with the client; it is not suggested as a response to be used often or early in a relationship.

Case One

Jack, the president of a small family-owned business, hired me to work with him and his two brothers in the development of their growing organization. Much of the initial work was spent in fairly lengthy sessions with Jack alone that consisted mainly of emotional statements by him as to what was wrong with his brothers and other managers. Jack paced up and down my office and frequently spoke in tones that could be heard by my partner and others in their offices. Most of the time, I sat quietly and listened, occasionally offering a nondirective acknowledgment or a question aimed at clarification. After several of these sessions, Jack began to ask me for advice and for suggestions as to action plans for remedying the situation. For the next few sessions, I resisted offering too many concrete suggestions but, from time to time, I did make more content-oriented responses. I began to feel Jack's growing restlessness and his irritation with my noncommital attitude. This culminated in a session in which he paced up and down my office and told me in no uncertain terms how useless I was as a consultant. I took this as long as I could but finally I jumped out of my chair and began to shout back that I was tired of his pacing and his tirades, that he didn't listen to anything I said, and that I felt sorry for him because he had so little frustration tolerance. I am generally soft-spoken and mild-mannered, and my colleagues expressed surprise when they told me later that the shouting carried into several other offices. After about five minutes of my shouting and dominating the exchange, he suddenly sat down, a huge grin crossed his face, and he said, "This is the first time in years that anyone has responded to me with any vigor."

Shortly after this session, I initiated a series of meetings with the three brothers—each of whom I had been meeting with individually up to that time. (It may be useful to point out that I made a decision to work up to group meetings because my initial assessment of the situation was that they needed to first heighten and expand their awareness around the ways they avoided or could not talk well with one another.) These were very difficult sessions, and progress as a group was very slow. If I encouraged the other brothers to share their thoughts and feelings, Jack interrupted them or made disparaging remarks about their contributions. I continued meeting with them individually during this time. In the sessions with Jack, I negotiated a rhythm in which we took turns listening to each other while pacing up and down or sitting quietly. My aim was to support his domineering behavior while showing him that both he and I were capable of listening, as well as bellowing. My job was to be true to my values about listening and to show him that this was a useful behavior. After about 18 months, during which all the brothers also attended several "stranger" sensitivity training sessions, I began to note a small shift in their interactions. Jack listened more and let the others speak. One of the brothers developed a more forthright, firm stance and learned to hold his ground against Jack. This earned Jack's grudging respect. Over a four-year period, this group became less contentious and more effective, but the basic dynamics prevailed and Jack remained somewhat domineering. The brothers learned that they could discuss issues well enough to run a successful business, even though they never did eliminate their negative feelings about each other.

In this case, consultant presence was an important element in getting all three brothers interested in the possibility that our work together might be fruitful. By providing some missing behaviors, a model is developed that evokes hope that growth or change is possible. In this instance, several critical behaviors were added:

1. For Jack, listening and patience in general were foreign. His brothers feigned listening but really tuned him out; the consultant was clearly interested.
2. Jack never had received an aggressive response to his diatribes. Arguing back was a relatively new experience for him.
3. For the other brothers, consultant firmness with Jack provided a model of how to stand up to him. In addition, frequent statements from the consultant that encouraged them to respond to Jack, or that encouraged Jack to ask them for statements of their thoughts or feelings, gave them support that was previously lacking.

This case shows that the Gestalt orientation is clearly that of process consultation, with the consultant endeavoring to focus client energy on its functioning and the way the system approaches its problems, rather than to make detailed analytical investigations and recommendations of preferred solutions. With the Cycle of Experience as an orienting principle, this leads to strong focus on awareness of oneself and the sharing of what is happening internally, as well as what seems to be occurring in the client system. Gestalt-oriented consulting broadens the usefulness of emotional expression and the sharing of one's own humanity in a variety of ways, counting very heavily on the forces of modeling and expectancy to create interest on the part of the client. In this approach it is very important to show respect for the system's way of being, while at the same time working very hard to highlight one's own way of being. In this way consultant differences can be more readily added to what is currently acceptable to the client, rather than be seen as jarring or evaluative.

BASIC ACTIVITIES OF A GESTALT-ORIENTED INTERVENTIONIST

The basic intervention behaviors drawing upon a Gestalt perspective are gleaned by following the flow of the Cycle of Experience, beginning with sensation and awareness. The five major activities may be listed as follows:

1. To attend, observe, and selectively share observations of what you see, hear, feel, etc., and thus establish your presence in so doing.
2. To attend to one's own experience (feelings, sensations, thoughts) and to selectively share these, thus establishing your presence in doing so.
3. To focus on energy in the client system and the emergence or lack of themes or issues (common figures) for which there is energy; to act to support mobilization of client energy (joining) so that something happens.
4. To facilitate clear, meaningful, heightened contacts between members of the client system (including their contact with you).
5. To help the group achieve heightened awareness of its overall process in completing units of work, and to learn to complete units of work so as to achieve closure around problem areas of unfinished business.

These fundamental activities of the consultant are exactly the skills that a Gestalt-oriented intervenor wishes to have the client system learn. Thus, while the consultant may design special learning "exercises" or serve as an observer of the ongoing activities of the client, a primary means of teaching is through the display of personal behavior. It is this emphasis, more than anything else, that gives the Gestalt perspective its unique flavor.

These activities make up the essential ingredients of the consultation process. Each has to do with some aspect of tuning into or attending to what is going on in the system, and then moving from this into support of available energy and effective action. The endeavor is to give the client a sense of the nature of good process and a way of better understanding the characteristic interruptions and blockages to good process that develop in that system. Following from this, the client then has the responsibility for making choices related to newly perceived awareness. This may or may not result in a decision to alter the structure and processes through which the system carries out its tasks.

The first two of the above activities—observing self and other and selectively sharing one's experience—are the cornerstones of Gestalt-oriented consultation. These are the behaviors that make the other three activities possible. To perform these behaviors well the consultant must become a well-honed instrument of observation and articulation. This suggests that development of self is the single most useful means of becoming an effective consultant. Yet, even with a high level of personal skill, selective sharing is a sensitive art. The next case illustrates how difficult this task can be.

Case Two

> This was an instance in which being "true" to the Gestalt perspective of sharing experience helped to create a difficult situation. Together with two male and one female colleagues, I was involved in an intensive team-building week with 50 people—all of whom were female. These individuals made up a university department of dietetics and nutrition and the dietetics staff of the teaching hospital associated with this ma-

jor medical school. In the first of many small group sessions, with each of the consultants as a facilitator, I said that I had never facilitated a group comprised exclusively of females before and that, while I was excited about it, I was feeling some concern about how well things would go. For the next two days, every time I met with this group, they would ask how I was feeling, and "hoped" that I was over my anxiety. No matter how often I assured them that I was fine and was only trying to set a norm for sharing feelings by making my earlier statement, I could not alleviate their concern.

When not focusing their concern on me, the group devoted much of the time to deflecting away from work issues and discussing such things as women's fashions, food recipes, and so forth. They seemed to be making things both easy and hard for me. Presumably I had nothing to contribute to the content, and there were no problems that required my assistance. For two or three sessions, I sat quietly after experiencing the force of this thrust, but then I began to interrupt the dialogue. I became more and more adamant in expressing that something was being avoided and that we had either to find out jointly what it was or accept the possibility that our work together would not be helpful to them or their organizations. After much twisting and turning, it was gradually revealed that I was seen as another of those "male physician types" who dominate their work world, and that they were simply dealing with me in the only way they knew how to experience power with these men. Some said that they didn't take me seriously because no doctor had ever shared any discomfort with them. Following this I became an invited observer of a most illuminating discussion about doctor–dietician relationships, male–female issues, and the power of the underdog. The women told me that they almost never articulated these thoughts with professional men of any kind. After this discussion, the group decided to deal with the work issues that had precipitated these team-building sessions.

Several considerations emerge from this example. First, selectively sharing one's experience can cause problems when the timing is bad or the cultural assumptions of the clients vary greatly from those of the consultant. Just as the Gestalt precept of sharing personal awareness often leads to useful responses by the client system, its actualization can create reactions not anticipated or desired by the consultant. Second, the key factor is not the immediate reaction to the expression of one's feelings, but that consultant interventions must energize the system in a way that ultimately leads to some learning by the system. This means that the consultant needs to have faith in a process that unfolds over time, including belief that the client system wants to experience feelings of competence and to achieve useful outcomes to problems—even when the system seems "resistant." In this case we did some very useful work eventually, and my being different may have had a positive long-term effect.

GESTALT APPROACH TO RESISTANCE

Another basic feature of a Gestalt model of intervention is the special definition of resistance and the way of dealing with it. The Gestalt-oriented consultant assumes as a working hypothesis that there is a great deal of ambivalence regarding change in any system. We assume that, even when people ask for help, there is energy in them that is directed against acceptance of help from others. This is no different than the seminal findings of Freud that desperate clients who sought him out against great obstacles presented him with enormous resistance as he tried to help them. The difference in a Gestalt approach is that this ambivalence is seen as a normal, potentially useful state, and there is great value in the client having strong forces against change even when it believes that the system can function better if some changes are made.

This perspective leads to respect for, and the acceptance of, client resistance. The job of a Gestalt-oriented interventionist is not to ensure that changes take place, but to help the client system *to heighten its awareness of the forces acting for and against its moving to a new place on a problem or an issue.* Thus the basic activities are employed to help the client to see what its resistance or ambivalence is. *The aim of the consultant is to help the system resolve the dilemmas that underlie that ambivalence.* The job is not to annihilate the resistance but to see that it is handled responsibly by the client. The Gestalt-oriented consultant does this by directing detailed attention to the manifestations of resistance and objections to doing something, as well as arguments for changing. Examination of the current state is essential, so that the client knows and acknowledges this reality. To make such an examination is to realize that there are positive forces for keeping things as they are, and that to change means more than giving up resistance.

Resistance is seen as strength, a force to be respected; the protective, curative, creative aspects of resistance are emphasized in this framework. Chapter 8 deals with this topic in greater detail. At this point it suffices to say that the Gestalt approach to resistance works from what has been called the paradoxical theory of change (Beisser, 1970). This theory states that one must first fully experience what *is* before recognizing all the alternatives of what *may be*. A similar perspective is that of V. Frankl's (1969) "paradoxical intentions." In his approach clients are asked to exaggerate undesirable behavior or annoying symptoms. The goal of these methods is to heighten awareness and ownership of the unwanted behavior and, through this, enable the client system to determine whether and how it wants to change.

RELATION OF GESTALT MODEL TO MODELS DESCRIBED BY SCHEIN

To appreciate the Gestalt model better, it is useful to relate it to well-known models put forth by others. In his book *Process Consultation,* and in a later paper, Edgar Schein (1969, 1977) presents a very helpful way of looking at the models or goals of intervention. He identifies three models: (1) the purchase of expertise, (2) doctor–patient, and (3) process consultation. In the purchase-of-expertise approach, a client solicits a consultant for a very specific, clearly identified piece of work related to technical or task issues involved in the functioning of the organization. It is assumed that the client has made a correct diagnosis of the problem and that this has been accurately communicated to a consultant who has the appropriate skills to do the job. The client accepts the work and the responsibility for the potential consequences. Employment of a computer software consulting firm to design and install a system to improve inventory control is a good example of this approach.

The second model is referred to as the doctor–patient model. The consultant still carries the major burden for the solution to the problem but there is greater emphasis on involvement of the outsider at the diagnostic level. This assumes that the client group can reveal the correct information for the consultant to arrive at a diagnosis and that the client has the willingness and the skills to implement the "prescription" provided by the consultant. The practice of internal medicine has traditionally followed this model.

The third model, and the one that Schein emphasizes in his own work, is that of process consultation. Here it is assumed that the client needs help from, and will benefit from, participation in carrying out a joint diagnosis of the problem. It is assumed that the client is ultimately the only one who knows the form of solution or change that will work, and has the ability to implement the solution. The task is seen as increasing problem-solving skills for future use, in addition to solving the immediate problem. It is also assumed that acceptance of solutions will be high as a consequence of the involvement of the client from the start of the effort.

These models may be understood in terms of system boundary phenomena and can be related to the general discussion of intervenor/system relationship presented earlier. In the purchase of expertise, it is as though the client gives a "piece" of the system to an outsider for a period of time. This piece is then returned to the organization. In the doctor–patient model, the interventionist is let into the system, but only partially and with clear limitations as to areas to be investigated and the symptoms to be addressed. In the process consultation model, the consultant becomes a special member of the "family" for a period of time. In this case there is always a possibility that the boundary may close behind or around the intervenor, with pressure or attraction developing to become part of the system. In the purchase of expertise or the doctor–patient model, there is less chance that the consultant will become an integral, ongoing part of the system.

In his discussion of these models, Schein makes a strong case for the value of process consultation, and he points out some of the shortcomings of the other approaches. One of his main points is that the data needed to make an appropriate diagnosis of a problem are often embedded in an organization, and that clients by themselves are not able to articulate this information. Given this, the purchase-of-expertise model runs the risk of developing a solution to a poorly or inaccurately defined problem. (One of the reasons we frequently have a repair done at an auto shop only to have to bring the car back again may be that the mechanic responded to our limited articulation of the problem. As the repair process unfolds, we are able to provide further information.) There is a further problem with this model in that the client learns very little from the process. The expert "fixes" what is broken and returns it to us. This minimal involvement may make it hard for clients to muster energy to do the maintenance work necessary to see that it does not break again.

The situation is similar in the doctor–patient model but is complicated by the greater involvement of the consultant in the diagnosis of the problem, and by the client in carrying out the "prescription" for solution. This requires a high trust in each other by the client and the consultant; in the implementation of the purchase-of-expertise model, there is typically more emphasis on the need for the client to trust the expert. Schein would argue that the doctor–patient model rests very strongly on the relationships between client and consultant if it is to succeed.

The process consultation model attempts to deal with these problems by providing a means of making more and better data available, and a way of enabling the client–consultant relationship to develop over time. If we label the first aspect that of *awareness* development and the second that of *contact,* we can see that the Gestalt model is clearly aligned with process consultation. As process consultation, the Gestalt perspective gives the client a great deal of credit for having a constructive intent and some problem-solving skills. The Gestalt perspective also sees the client as needing educational experiences in order to be able to solve its own problems in the future. As indicated earlier, it may well be that the major difference between the Gestalt orientation and other process consultants is the extent to which a high-impact, interactional intervention style is employed. It is this aspect that is most often lacking in the purchase-of-expertise and doctor–patient models.

This discussion should not imply that the purchase-of-expertise and doctor–patient models have limited use, or that process consultation is the only valuable model. For certain complex, highly technical problems, the purchase-of-expertise model will be appropriate. Gestalt and other process models may be viewed as an addition to this approach. Most experts now agree that implementation of solutions is their biggest problem, not technical know-how. It is in dealing with implementation issues that the purchase-of-expertise consultant needs to do better in developing both client and consultant awareness throughout the entire assignment, beginning with assessment of the problem and design of the solution. This would surface the ambivalence of the client, as well as offer more data for diagnosis. Likewise, a compelling presence—one that inspires more interest than does simply being a top-notch technical expert—can help in generating client energy to ensure that the solution does indeed work.

In the case of the doctor–patient model, good process consultation skills can also make a contribution. Much organizational consulting is based on this model that falls somewhere between the more detached "expertise" model and the more involving process model, and may be seen as less disruptive to the organization. Most educational interventions fall into this category: there is a needs assessment ("diagnosis by the doctor"), followed by a specially designed intervention to deal with the problem uncovered (prescription). There is much value in these interventions when they are used to heighten awareness or teach a specific skill. As in the case of the "expertise" model, better, more thorough work at the awareness phase, and a more compelling presence during the teaching phase, will do much to increase the impact of these interventions.

RELATIONSHIP OF THE MODEL TO ARGYRIS' THEORY OF INTERVENTION

In a series of books, Chris Argyris has developed a model of organizational learning and intervention that has added considerably to the field of process consultation (Argyris, 1970; Argyris & Schon, 1978; Argyris, 1982, Argyris, 1985). Highly relevant to the Gestalt model is his statement of the key issues of intervention in *Intervention Theory and Practice* (1970). In this book he lays down three basic requirements of intervention.

1. The generation of valid data.
2. Free informed choice by the client, so that the client maintains autonomy.
3. The choices made by the client are done in such a way that internal commitment to these choices is high.

Argyris is quite clear and firm in maintaining that these three tasks are the only ones of consequence, and that the interventionist's role is to work with the client so that they may be achieved. He further states that the effectiveness of client functioning should be evaluated by means of the three criteria and, most important, that interventions must be based upon these requirements. He further states that the client should learn to do these three tasks, and that the modeling and teaching of the interventionist are crucial. With regard to change, Argyris makes an elegant case that this is not a primary task of the consultant, but is an option of the client that is based upon free informed choice, following the development of valid data.

Though Argyris developed his model from a different theoretical perspective than that of Gestalt therapy, the correspondence of his position with the Gestalt model is readily apparent. In Gestalt terminology the generation of valid data would be described as the enhancement of awareness leading to the emergence of clear figures around which there is some interest or energy. The tasks of informed choice and commitment clearly have to do with the action-contact phase of the Cycle of Experience. The client becomes energized as a result of the data/awareness and moves into an action in order to achieve some learning (completion of a unit of work). The Gestalt consultant would describe this as good contact and assimilation of the learning that follows from good contact. As with the Gestalt model, heightening of awareness about what might be labeled "resistance" is a major objective, but the decision to change remains the responsibility of the client.

In his subsequent writing, Argyris turned his attention more to a study of dysfunctional behavior in organizations. His conception of the difference between espoused theories and theories in action shows how organizations prevent change from occurring by choosing means of solving problems that do not force examination of basic values and assumptions (Argyris & Schon, 1978). In a later work (Argyris, 1985), he focuses on problems in strategy formulation and implementation caused by what he calls "defensive routines." For the consultant working from these perspectives, the task is clearly one of enhancing awareness in a group through sharing unspoken thoughts and feelings, and of getting the participants to share and test assumptions. This is very similar to the Gestalt approach to encouraging the client to articulate the assumptions underlying attitudes and behaviors that are both accepted and rejected by the system. Raimy (1976) has referred to this exploration as cognitive therapy, quoting extensively from a single therapy session in which Fritz Perls challenges a client 26 times to examine a single assumption. In his books Argyris provides detailed, often sentence-by-sentence accounts of client actions, and of his encouragement of client members to express whatever occurred to them that they had chosen not to say at that moment.

We see, then, that the Argyris model and the Gestalt model represent process consultation in its fullest sense. They are also alike in that they call for work at the microlevel of detailed, specific behavior. The major difference in the approaches lies in the way the consultant uses himself or herself. Argyris, as a dedicated researcher and theorist, stresses cognitive clarity and understanding through use of a systematic framework and incisive observation. In his approach the consultant is a more detached player than in the Gestalt orientation, employing less high-contact, personally revealing behavior as an instrument of change. Both models have the same objective and fundamental stress on the importance of awareness. The Gestalt approach puts more emphasis on energizing the client through personal, emotional involvement. What is more important than the differences, however, is how closely these models fit together even though developed from different initial perspectives.

IMPLICATIONS

The Gestalt model represents an extension of mainstream process consultation. Though derived primarily from work in the therapeutic arena, and with concentration upon individuals, the orientation underlying the Gestalt approach is readily applied to a powerful model of consultation. In applying this model, the Gestalt-oriented practitioner is in many ways similar to other organization consultants, using such approaches as data-based models of intervention, team development, and career planning as the technical means of implementing organization change. What is different, however, is the guideline or yardstick that remains in the foreground of the Gestalt practitioner in carrying out his or her work. The following questions are indicative of the orientation that guides the work and take precedence over investment in any particular technical or methodological aspect, or investment in outcomes of the interventions.

- Am I heightening the awareness of the client system with respect to its process in trying to deal with its problems?
- Does my intervention help to lead to the generation of awareness (data, or valid information) regarding the client's problems and ways of functioning?
- Am I establishing a presence during each stage of intervention that aids in the awareness/data generation/contact process?
- Does my intervention build upon the energy of the client system and what is currently a figural, workable theme or issue, or is it my "imposition" of a value or desired solution that guides the work?
- Does my intervention help to enhance the contacts between parts of the system and to provide learning about such things as subsystem boundaries and joint efforts for improving effectiveness?
- Do my interventions enhance the ability of the client to understand and employ the skills involved in the Cycle of Experience?
- What does this intervention do to my position relative to the system—where am I with regard to boundary and marginality issues? Am I getting in "enough," "too much," etc.?
- Am I furthering the development of the client's skills in seeing new ways of addressing system problems, particularly

heightening the awareness of what it is possible to achieve at any given moment? In other words, how much awareness is there of the value of keeping things as they are, versus enhancing the appreciation of the need for doing things differently?

This list is only representative of what follows from a pure process consultation model, and those who have been influenced by a group dynamics/field theory approach will raise very similar questions as guidelines to their practice. Again, the Gestalt-oriented practitioner not only raises these questions as orientation, but acts upon them in such a way that his or her presence results in a highly effective process though which the client develops the answers.

REFERENCES

Argyris, C. *Intervention Theory and Method.* Reading, Mass.: Addison-Wesley, 1970.

Argyris, C., and Schon, D. *Organizational Learning: A Theory of Action Perspective.* Reading, Mass.: Addison-Wesley, 1978.

Argyris, C. *Reasoning, Learning and Action.* San Francisco: Jossey-Bass, 1982.

Argyris, C. *Strategy Change and Defensive Routines.* Boston: Pitman Publishing, 1985.

Beisser, A. "The paradoxical theory of change." In J. Fagan and I. Sheperd (eds.), *Gestalt Therapy Now.* Palo Alto, Calif.: Science and Behavior Books, 1970.

Frankl, V. *The Will to Meaning.* Cleveland, Ohio: New American Library, 1969, (pp. 101–107).

Raimy, V. "Changing misconceptions as the therapeutic task." In A. Burton (ed.), *What Makes Behavior Change Possible.* New York: Brunner/Maazel, 1976.

Schein, E.H. *Process Consultation.* Reading, Mass.: Addison-Wesley, 1969.

Schein, E.H. "The role of the consultant: Content expert of process facilitator?" *Working Paper,* Sloan School of Management, 1977.

4 On Presence: The Consultant as a Learning Model

In earlier chapters two major themes were introduced, both of which are important to understanding organization intervention:

1. The Cycle of Experience: The role of the interventionist is to teach the client system those skills necessary for understanding the Cycle of Experience and for functioning better in carrying out the processes of awareness, contact, etc.
2. Presence: The role of the interventionist is to provide a presence that is otherwise lacking in the client system.

The full use of presence is a cornerstone of the Gestalt approach, and critical to its successful practice. The meaning and implication of this important notion are developed in this chapter. The concept of presence is seen as a key to understanding the educational model inherent in the Gestalt orientation.

The proposed framework considers presence as the living embodiment of knowledge: *the theories and practices believed to be essential to bring about change in people are manifested, symbolized, or implied in the presence of the consultant.* Assumptions about *what* to learn and *how* to learn in order to function more effectively are transformed into the behavior of the intervenor as he or she takes on a helping role with a client system. An understanding of the various ways this is manifested, and of how it takes place, is crucial to effective intervention. Indeed, it is possible to state that the way in which the consultant presents himself or herself to the client is a culminating statement of that person's view of the nature of good functioning. For a Gestalt-oriented consultant, the Cycle of Experience is the model of effective functioning.

Presence is a very difficult concept to define, evoking words such as power, influence, style, charisma, and the like. But it is not just an abstract concept; it is tangible, palpable, and can be seen and felt. Presence is *always* brought into the consulting setting, whether or not the bearer is aware of how it varies or is perceived. Presence is defined as:

> The living out of values in such a way that in "taking a stance," the intervenor *teaches* these important concepts. That which is important to the client's learning process is exuded through the consultant's way of being.

From this definition it should be understood that presence is not the same as style or personality which, though aspects of presence, are not sufficient to define its essence. Presence is a living-out of basic assumptions regarding how one influences or helps another. These assumptions can be explicitly displayed in one's presence, or the presence can exude mystery and demand that the client work to understand the assumptions and eventually gain insight. Style is a more superficial—albeit important—aspect of presence. Style is the delivery of the message. Style alone cannot account for what is meant when someone says: "Consultant X has a strong presence." Presence denotes a good integration of knowledge and behavior. By making here-and-now behavior an enactment of what the person knows, presence becomes a powerful force. The more compelling or intriguing the knowledge and its enactment, the richer is the presence. Style may add to enactment, but it is simply a display of charm unless it accompanies an internalized body of knowledge.

Understanding the difference between presence and style is crucial to an understanding of the power of the truly potent change agent in all walks of life, including leaders and managers, as well as healers of all persuasions. In a recent article in *Fortune* magazine about Chrysler Corporation and Lee Iacocca's success in turning it around (Flax, 1985), mention is made of a large meeting to introduce a new car in November 1984:

> Chrysler invited the plant's 2300 hourly workers, many called back recently from layoffs and retrained to operate new equipment, to watch with the usual political and industry bigwigs and journalists. When Iacocca stepped out of the glistening silver Dodge Lancer he had driven into the spotlight, those workers let out a roar worthy of the crowds in Latin American soccer stadiums when their national teams take the field. There wasn't an atom of ambiguity about who they were working for—the man whom they believed saved their jobs, their mortgages, their children's tuition.

To look at this incident and conclude that Iacocca has a powerful personality or "great style" is correct, but it misses the core of his essence as a change agent: Without an underlying vision and a theory of how to engage people in saving a dying corporation—one that he was living out in his actions—he would not be seen as a great presence. His power lies in the complete incorporation of his beliefs and assumptions about change into his behavior. Another individual may have had a similar vision of how to save Chrysler, but lacked the skills to transform this vision into a commanding presence. Vision and style must be well integrated for presence to matter.

We can see this phenomenon in effective teachers, those individuals who have internalized and mastered their subject matter and can "live it" in their daily behavior. My own interest in Shakespeare and in theater in general was kindled by a high school teacher who, on the first day of a course in English literature, put her chair on top of her desk, climbed onto the chair, and proceeded to perform Act I, Scene I, of *Macbeth* (the witches' scene), while the class sat riveted by her presentation. What Ms. Shirley conveyed was not simply an eccentricity of style, but the important point that Shakespeare wrote words to be spoken aloud to an audience. Without a theory of the play, of the theater, and of how to teach these theories, she would have been experienced as a caricature or as a bit weird, rather than as a powerful catalyst for creating interest in theater.

Three cases from my consulting practice show that presence does not require a dramatic quality to have impact. The requirements in the first two cases were similar in that both settings involved groups of managers who were not accustomed to working intimately with each other and who were brought together in a tense atmosphere.

Case One

About ten years ago, I was engaged in a very sensitive team-building consultation involving the senior executives of two organizations that had just been merged. I was known to the executives of both firms, as I had been consulting with both organizations prior to the merger (for two years in the case of one firm and about seven years in the other). One group was located on the West Coast; the other was headquartered in an eastern city, where the surviving corporate office was to be located. Though all concerned had been assured that no jobs would be eliminated and that the West Coast office would be maintained for some years, there was a great deal of tension, mistrust, and suspicion among the ten executives involved. Rather than contract for off-site sessions, which would have been a radical and potentially explosive move for this group, I elicited an agreement from the chairman of the board and the president (each representing one of the premerger firms) to hold ongoing monthly meetings of all the senior people at the eastern headquarters. These were to be working sessions in which part of the time would be devoted to corporate-level issues such as financing and strategy, and part to a monthly operations review. I was to be the consultant to the process and to attend each meeting. In addition, I was to use my judgment to arrange meetings between sessions with any of the executives, singly or in combinations, for issues requiring interdependent action or conflict resolution.

The newly promoted executive vice president was to run the operations-review portion of the meeting. The chairman and the president were to be jointly responsible for the other portion. Neither of these men was highly skilled at running meetings and they tended to operate from loose agendas that avoided public confrontation. I was asked by both men to help in running the meetings and not to be simply an observer or process consultant. I agreed to do one task that seemed consistent with the fact that the group knew I was the architect of the meeting concept: for the first few meetings, I would start the session by generating the agenda with the group and helping them develop priorities for discussion. A memo concerning any critical issue that had to be dealt with would be sent out to participants in advance, with supporting information. Otherwise we were to develop the agenda at the meeting.

Another approach might have been to start with a more intense interaction, so that the group could proceed directly to sensitive interpersonal issues. Perhaps the strategy chosen was too cautious and allowed a great deal of concern or negative feeling to remain unsurfaced. It is also possible that the agenda-building role was inappropriate. In any case, I knew that I had to be especially careful in this setting, and that by dealing with work issues the group might begin to trust each other and learn to put difficult matters on the table over a period of time. Two aspects were of primary concern to me in this consideration: (1) I had to start where the client was ready to begin; (2) I was the only person in the room who was trusted by everyone else. Could I use myself as a model of calmness and objectivity, perhaps modeling a role otherwise missing? Would this presence evoke a greater feeling of trust over a period of time and avoid the possible damage of a more provocative approach?

Starting each meeting by standing at an easel and acting as a catalyst, I performed this role for a period of six sessions. It soon became clear that this was no longer necessary and that the group was able to initiate its agenda as soon as the president called the meeting to order. A lot of other work took place over an 18-month period to build this team as a new entity, but a total group off-site meeting was never held. Much of my work between sessions was geared to get people to work together and to feel free to bring up agenda items at the monthly meetings. Two years later this management group was working at a high level of effectiveness and only one executive had left because of a personality clash. The same management group was operating a very successful organization five years later.

Case Two

Recently, as part of my work with the president and executive vice president of a major division of an electronics firm, I assisted in the design and conduct of a four-day retreat involving the top 23 managers of the firm. I had started consulting in this situation seven months earlier, when the two top executives asked me to help them build their relationship as an "office of the president." These men had taken over their jobs about six months prior to this, following a reorganization in the company—a move based in part on a decision to eliminate severe intergroup competitiveness and strong clique formation. This major change had not been fully implemented and there was a need for further refinement within the division, and for development of a new strategic plan. Some pockets of bad feeling still existed from the reorganization. The immediate impetus for the retreat was a restructuring of roles and reporting relationships, which the president and executive vice president had put into effect a month before the meeting.

It was decided that the retreat would be a stretegic planning session that would be built around a process being developed by the planning manager and his strategy consultant, and which would result in steps to further this process. While various attendees had worked on different aspects of this process, they had not done so since the recent restructuring, nor had these managers ever participated in a planning meeting as a total group. The design for the meeting was very simple: all the participants were asked to come to the meeting prepared to discuss several planning questions or issues pertinent to their immediate responsibility and to the objectives of the division as a whole. About half of them were asked to prepare short presentations focusing on an overview of their area, such as marketing, finance, operations, or research and development. All of this was arranged for by the president and executive vice president, with the help of their planning people. I had no input with respect to content, nor did I have any contact with the other attendees, with the exception of the planning manager. Some of the attendees were aware of my work with top management but they did not know me prior to the retreat.

The meeting was started by the president and executive vice president. The design called for a rhythm of presentations and small work groups composed of people now related as a function of the recent restructuring. My participation consisted largely of explaining the schedule, acting as timekeeper, sitting in on sessions as an observer, and making occasional comments but only to help in clarifying what was being communicated. I met with the president and executive vice president one evening to help them plan the final session. In addition, I ate with and chatted with participants during free time.

I cannot think of another occasion in which I played such a low-key role. I gave no formal presentations and did not engage in strong actions to promote high contact. What I provided was a structure and a calming presence designed to give the participants—including the president and executive vice president—reassurance that what might have been a very difficult, troublesome meeting could be carried off well. At its conclusion, people who had not worked together before said that they appreciated getting to know each other, and several said that it was the best meeting they had attended since joining the company. Seven important action items were identified, with a follow-up session to review plans by appointed task forces scheduled for six weeks later.

This meeting represented just a beginning. My presence, embodying the belief that people will learn how to be more effective if there is a positive expectation that they can do so—and if good supportive structures for learning are provided, made it possible to start the process.

Case Three

After working for several years with an organization that changed very little during this time, I blithely asked the top executives why they continued to ask for (and pay for) my services when it appeared that I had little or no contribution to make. The reply from the chairman of the board was, "But you don't understand! Just think how much worse things would be if you were not available to us?"

In following up on this intriguing remark, I was told by other managers at different levels that, when I appeared, the atmosphere was calmer, people seemed more at ease with each other, and they were less tired after meetings. It became apparent that my presence evoked reassurance about who they were and how they operated, which they may not yet have been able to provide for themselves.

PRESENCE IN TEACHING

The examples in this and the preceding chapter show that the power of presence is sometimes highlighted in specific dramatic actions, but it also derives from general or diffuse patterns of behavior. The ways in which ideas are expressed, the quality of energy displayed, and the perceived values of an individual all contribute to presence. Presence is not manufactured; it is something everyone displays at all times, whether one is aware of what others respond to or not. However, presence is most powerful when it embodies a compelling model or theory of learning. While some learning models are more useful than others in influencing adult behavior change, the important point is that the consultant has internalized one that has proven useful over time.

The model of Hassidic teachings used by the zaddikim is illuminating in this regard. In *The Early Masters*, Martin Buber (1975) discusses the nature of these teachings and how they are passed down in the form of legendary stories by and about the zaddikim, a group of religious leaders who appeared among European Jews in the 17th century. As Buber shows, the single incident of each of these legendary stories conveys the meaning of life. In this theory of education, story telling is a cornerstone. Each zaddik acts as a guide in his followers' search to understand better how to deal with their existence and everyday problems. The stories contain a wide variety of content or metaphor, yet the core message is that life can be managed if the individual maintains fervor in caring about what matters and can sustain an exalted joy. The "theory of education" from which the zaddik works eschews proselytizing or preaching. As Buber (1975) indicates: "The zaddik strengthens his hassid [follower] in his hours of doubting but does not infiltrate him with truth." Whether a given zaddik has one style or another—the variety of zaddikim personality styles is amply demonstrated in Buber's profiles in this and other books—it is the combination of style and an actualized theory of learning that lends power to his presence. When a zaddik says: "I learned the Torah from all the limbs of my teacher," we gain insight into how the powerful presence of the teacher emerges from this integration.

STYLE AS AN ELEMENT OF PRESENCE

Style refers to the unique way in which an individual combines such things as voice, words, gestures, dress or costume, emotional tone, and general manner. One's style is an important aspect of presence. We have only to look at how different people enter a situation, and how they introduce themselves, to see how important style is in the creation of presence. But to concentrate on *manner* as though it is equivalent to presence is to look only at coloration, or to build a theory of influence around the kind of data that inform first impressions. Unless manner and the ideology around how to influence others together form a strong, coherent whole, the resulting presence will lack power. If we look at Jesse Jackson or President Reagan, and pay attention to the way they use language, their general manner, and so forth, we can see clear distinctions in their very different styles. Their styles aid the enactment of what they believe in and they emerge as powerful presences. Each has developed a presence in which there is total congruence of ideology around human nature and social change and the way in which he expresses himself. One might speculate that President Carter was less effective as a leader because he did not achieve an integration of style and a theory of change that resulted in a compelling presence, or that the integration he did accomplish was too much in violation of the expectations of people for him to have high impact.

Interest on the part of helping professionals in the power of style as an aspect of presence was enhanced about 25 years ago, with the coming of age of existential therapies and the human potential movement. The growth of the encounter group movement and the profession of organization development fostered many experiments in intervenor style and led to a broadening of conceptions of the effective stance of the helping professional. However, confusion in distinguishing between style and presence resulted in a popular view that presence emerged out of the full expression of what/who one is. "Being who I am," "letting it all hang out," and "sharing fully and honestly" became rallying cries for many. Professional development programs and organizational interventions took a turn away from emphasis on the role of theory, particularly rejecting those assumptions related to more orthodox schools of thought. The pendulum swung away from what may have been an overly rational, intellectual approach and moved toward emphasis on here-and-now exchanges with clients. While some correction was clearly necessary, the pendulum appears to have gone too far in favor of emphasizing expressiveness and emotional reeducation as the key to improving effectiveness in human systems. In no little way, the ability to "free clients up," to be charismatic, or otherwise to model spontaneity and individuality became a theory of individual and organizational change. Many helping professionals seemed to have forgotten the importance of *meaning* if the client was truly to assimilate and learn from the powerful experiences being created. It is interesing, in this regard, that the Yalom and Lieberman (1973) study of the effectiveness of different styles of encounter group leadership showed that those group leaders who emphasized an approach in which the client was able to complete an "educational" experience by drawing some personal meaning out of it, achieved significantly better results than charismatic leaders or those who did not. While some have questioned the design of this study, since the time of its publication there has been a shift toward a better integration of experiential approaches with more conceptual orientations toward organizational learning.

PRESENCE IN THE GESTALT FRAMEWORK

To summarize the argument thus far: Presence emerges out of and is experienced as an integration of a well-conceived and assimilated theoretical base and a way of presenting oneself that actualizes this theory of learning or change. In effect, the intervenor becomes the embodiment of the theory. The nature of this integration and how it is accomplished determines the quality and power of the presence.

Given the above perspective, we can turn to an analysis of what presence means in a Gestalt framework, and of how it is manifested by effective practitioners. If a major goal of the Gestalt-oriented consultant is to provide a presence that is missing in the client system, what kinds of presences are useful, and what are the theoretical assumptions that help to determine what is useful? And if the role of the consultant is to help the client system learn skills, how does presence aid in this endeavor?

The answers to these questions come from consideration of two requirements of an effective helping relationship:

1. The need for the consultant to be interesting enough to achieve and maintain engagement with the client system.
2. The need to understand where in the Cycle of Experience the client system is functioning ineffectively or can benefit from enhanced awareness or skill development.

The first of these requirements involves presentation of self by the consultant in such a way that interest develops by the client in undertaking a study to understand its process better. This rests on having a compelling or intriguing presence, on creating client curiosity about both the consultant and the client system itself. Without an effective presence at this point it is doubtful that a solid contract between intervenor and client can be developed. Ineffective presence at this point most likely leads to short-term or aborted contracts. Without some minimum level of contact, some degree of being "touched" by the consultant, the system probably will not mobilize to learn. This is a readiness-to-learn phase. While it may seem to the inexperienced practitioner that style is the main element in the success of this phase of the work, unless a vision of what is possible to learn is displayed by the consultant—even in rudimentary form—the potency of his or her presence will be limited. The exception to this is the rare phenomenon of the highly charismatic intervenor who is spellbinding enough to grab the attention of the client by a delivery or "performance" that is seen as a complete education or a learning experience merely by being witnessed.

The second requirement directs us toward *what* is to be taught by the intervenor and/or learned by the client system. This requires consultant skills in awareness, energy mobilization, contact enhancement, and so forth, as well as a general perspective toward living in and learning from the present moment and attractive values. From this emerges a coherence, an integrity composed of much more than a facile display of charm and intelligence.

This requirement calls for a practitioner who has internalized the Cycle of Experience as an orienting principle through experiencing it as both a client and a consultant. One must not only believe intellectually that this theory of awareness is a powerful perspective, one must have assimilated the value of the awareness process into his or her *visceral* and *skeletal* being as a fundamental biological orientation. In this way the awareness model becomes the foundation to which style is added to create presence.

To a large extent, how this integration takes place is a mystery, as all assimilation processes are hard to grasp. One experiences a strong presence with a sense of appreciation as one would have for a fine work of art: in either instance it is very difficult to provide a detailed analysis of components that together add up to the total experience. Yet we can identify some skills of presentation and a sense of aesthetics for artists, and we do have useful educational experiences for training and developing them. There is no reason to doubt that this can be done for systems consultants, who practice an art form of a different quality than, say, painters.

To comprehend the full meaning of presence, it may help to look at studies of healers, sages, gurus, and others. Analyses of Buddha (unidentified author, 1974) and Confucius (Legge, date unknown), and the writings of Martin Buber (1947, 1975), Elie Weisel (1973), Sheldon Kopp (1971, 1972), and Joseph Adelson (1961) are relevant in this regard. We are told about the shaman, the guru, the sage, the priest, the magician, the zaddik, the mystic healer, the naturalist, and so on. Confucius is considered a sage, and "the follower of Confucius, having looked into his heart to find the right path, would then be governed by the rules of 'right conduct' " (Legge). Buddha, a sage and, as with Confucius, a believer of no theology, "does not tell why we live, but how to live. He teaches a way of life, a way to rise above the troubles of life finally to achieve the ultimate happiness of Nirvana. . . ."(1974). The guru, on the other hand, is seen as "strange to all rule and tradition," as a "spiritual guide" or "one who gives religious instruction." Kopp (1971) quotes Parcelsus as saying that "a guru should not tell the naked truth," a dictum that pushes toward a different presence than that of the more revealing sage. As with the guru, the shaman (perhaps they are one and the same) works through complex metaphors and uses costumes, props, and rituals to suggest knowledge hidden from ordinary people. Kopp reminds us that shamanism originally meant the spontaneous losing of the self.

The magician seems to stress the rituals of the shaman. The modern-day naturalist is like a sage who has the benefit of science and empiricism (e.g., the physician). The zaddik, as indicated earlier, seems to fall somewhere in between the sage and the guru, helping his followers to find the "right path," but guiding them to find it through stories rich in metaphor.

An examination of the various approaches represented by these "wise men," as well as highly impactful change agents in all walks of life, indicates that several factors determine the source of their power:

- *"Rightness."* An almost universal sense of feeling at home in being a performer (in the best sense of the term), with an appreciation for the skills of timing, modulation, projection, etc.
- *Being explicit versus being mysterious.* The ability to present a strong stance along the continuum which at one end emphasizes reason, the knowable, the empirical—that which can be made explicit—versus mystery, the intuitive, or the "imaginative," at the other end.
- *Narcissistic versus collective identity.* The ability to present a strong stance along the continuum of which one end stresses a narcissistic orientation, focusing attention on the "sage" and his or her *personal gifts*, versus an orientation in which the attention is focused on the "sage" as a *representative or member* of an important group or school of thought.
- *Clinical versus contactful mode.* The ability to present a strong stance along the continuum which, at one end, stresses an emotionally neutral, "clinical" mode, with emphasis on detachment so that correct diagnosis and solution of problems can be made, versus emphasis on the value of being present with the learner, and on the excitement of "taking a journey together."

While there may be other important factors, these are some of the core issues to examine if one is to understand presence. These are the factors that bind together one's learning objectives and one's individuality of expression.

RIGHTNESS

The sense of being a skilled performer may be a prerequisite to the other factors. Those who have presence in the eyes of others appear to be doing and being what they are meant to be. Neither apology nor self-consciousness is manifested in their manner, nor do they employ the exaggerations of a pretender or role player. Whether shy and introverted or outgoing and extroverted, their presence conveys a *right* to be where they are. [It may well be that this is the most important factor in the presence of the zaddik; according to Buber (1975), the term means "the proven" or "one who has stood the test," implying an earned right to this presence.] There is no doubt that the greatest single factor in Iacocca's success at Chrysler is that he was perceived from the beginning as the perfect person to do the job. Among well-known organizational consultants, Richard Beckhard's presence is abundant in its "rightness." In the area of social change, Martin Luther King and Saul Alinsky were seen as "having stood the test." World-class psychotherapists of all persuasions exude this in their presence.

"Rightness" is one of the hardest aspects to teach an inexperienced consultant. It involves being able to transcend anxiety about what is happening and what to do about it, and when achieved, results in compelling, interesting behavior, not in perfection. Once achieved, good timing and pacing of interventions come out of an intuitive sense of appropriateness rather than that of trial and error searching. "Mistakes" will occur but will be experienced as the inevitable part of a total process, rather than as inexperienced fumbling with identity and presentation of self.

BEING EXPLICIT VERSUS BEING MYSTERIOUS

The second factor, the preference for the explicit versus the mysterious, separates the sage/naturalist from the guru/mystic healer type of intervenor. The sage/naturalist approach is based on wise, judicious use of knowledge, laws, and that which can be codified. This perspective stresses analysis, diagnosis, and the use of normative, prescriptive solutions. The making of connections and the interpretation of phenomena are frequent behaviors of this intervenor, and are seen as the skills to be acquired by the client. In short, the presence of the sage/naturalist has as its core value the highest expression of empirical knowing. In this sense, it is the lessons of the past, the "wisdom of the ages," that defines the aura around the sage/naturalist.

By contrast, the guru/mystic healer focuses more on that which is less obvious and less readily seen or felt. The mode is a more poetic one, rich in metaphor and symbols of all kinds. Teaching is done through the use of dilemma, paradox, and the conundrum, rather than through the linear-associative method of the sage/naturalist. Working with dreams and fantasies comes easily to the guru/mystic healer, and clients are taught to be highly respectful of their own fantasies. If the sage/naturalist uses the past to make probabilistic predictions of the future, the guru/mystic healer will employ prophecy that may have little direct relationship to observable, external events, but that stems from apparent submission to an internal vision. The guru/mystic healer takes a cosmological viewpoint toward existence, seeking to expand and transcend boundaries; the sage/naturalist is more interested in exploring and teaching that which is manageable by human beings.

The above perspectives are readily seen in the presence of well-known organization development practitioners. Edgar Schein, Chris Argyris, and Harry Levinson are examples of individuals who have developed highly impactful presences stemming in large part from a stance close to the sage/naturalist end of the continuum. The way in which these intervenors work with respect to organization assessment is discussed in Chapter 6. Though the guru/mystic healer is less likely to be seen in organizational consultants, we see it in those who have been influenced by Eastern philosophy, Suffiism, and so forth. Carl Whitaker, a well-known family therapist, is compelling in his way of being imaginative or mysteriouus with clients. Paul Goodman is an excellent example of one who internalized a workable combination of both in his presence, using his extensive knowledge in various areas to demonstrate his wisdom, and also using poetic modes in an impressive manner. Will Schutz and Elaine Kepner draw power in their presence from being able to show both sides of this continuum.

NARCISSISTIC VERSUS COLLECTIVE IDENTITY

The third factor, the preference for a narcissistic identity versus a collective identity, has to do with whether the presence exhibited focuses on personal, unique qualities as the source of power, or personification of a discipline or subject matter adhered to by many is seen to be the source of influence. As Adelson [1961] points out, there are many different collectivities and, thus, a variety of stances to be taken. Identification with psychoanalysis, and a stance based on an image of how the ideal psychoanalyst should behave, will lead to a presence that is different from one based on identification with Skinnerian behavior modification or cultural anthropology. Therefore, one may reject, suppress, or ignore the value that comes from belonging to a group or a school of thought in favor of the values residing inside oneself. The narcissistic presence directs attention to the consultant, and we learn by observing this intervenor in action as he or she engages ideas and people in a fascinating and attractive way.

A fiercely proud, independent quality is exuded in the narcissistic presence, and learners often respond to or identify with this surface manifestation, rather than to the underlying struggle and ingenuity required to achieve such autonomy. The reaction of many people to Fritz Perls is an example of how the unsophisticated student can miss this distinction. People responded to Perls' performance characteristics, to the "I do my thing, you do your thing" aspect rather than to the core of his stance. If one tried to learn through *being* with Fritz Perls, rather than by trying to *imitate* him, what one learned—perhaps better than from anyone else—was that *if one is willing to pay the price in pain, loneliness, and the like, it is possible to learn to be your own person and to stand fully for what you believe, both professionally and in personal life.* Thus the problem in learning from the narcissistic presence comes only when one tries to become a "carbon copy" and measures all learning progress against the master being copied. However, when seen as but one very attractive, vividly portrayed life, this consultant can be a true source of inspiration to the learner.

By contrast, an orientation toward collective identity will stress the value of being what one stands for and will emphasize a discipline or an orthodoxy. Adelson (1961) refers to this as being the presence of "the priest." This approach tends to support a more impersonal manner, with much less self-revelation than found among the more narcissistically oriented presence. As with the sage/naturalist, with whom this perspective is closely allied, the presence of this consultant is an embodiment of the importance of concepts, subject matter, and, presumably, a tried-and-true doctrine. The advantage of this presence is that the learner sees a solid theory in action and is not subject to the conflict and confusion that might exist without the support that comes from a consensually agreed upon body of knowledge. The problem with the presence of this intervenor is that it tends to give the client a message that flexibility or nonconformity in applying the particular doctrine will seriously impair learning. Thus the practice of an established craft is the message of the collectively oriented intervenor, whereas the narcissistic intervenor's presence indicates that powerful personal impact is more important than possessing a particular badge or membership card.

CLINICAL VERSUS CONTACTFUL MODE

The fourth factor, preference of an objective, "clinical" mode, versus being emotionally involved and joining the client's exploration, helps to define the distinction between many Gestalt-oriented consultants and those who work from the purchase-of-expertise model. At one end of the continuum, the emphasis is on detachment. The consultant is not personally involved to a great extent, but draws power from dispassionate curiosity and an austere manner that promises unflinching integrity when done well. At the other end is more passionate involvement, with greater expression of feelings and personal experiences. There is likely to be strong identification with the client system, or with certain members of the system (this can become a problem if a strong bond develops). The clinical mode has an advantage in this regard, as it prevents dysfunctional confluence from taking place in the consultant-client relationship. It also allows the consultant to say difficult things, using "hard" data as support and not being deterred by emotional concerns.

Since organizations are generally task-oriented and use consultants to alleviate specific symptoms, there is often a strong pull toward the clinical mode. In response, numerous practitioners have developed a presence that implies that things can be fixed within a reasonable time frame. The clinical mode implies that, given the right facts, diagnosis and remedy will be readily forthcoming. The contactful presence tends to be less focused and to promise less by way of specific outcomes. Rather, it relies on development of great trust in the apparent depth of commitment by the consultant to stay with the client through what may be a difficult struggle. Carl Rogers is masterful in drawing on this ability.

CONCLUSION

In reviewing the above factors, it is important to recognize that underlying each position are basic, strongly held assumptions about what best produces learning by the client system. Whether it is in providing a collective or narcissistic identity, being explicit or mysterious, or being "clinical" or contactful, consultant presence stands for educational values and principles. In discussing the modes, support has been given for all of the stances, and advocating one form of presence over another has been avoided. A case has been made for understanding presence as the integration of a theory of learning or influence with individual expression in such a way that the intervenor actualizes important values and ways of being in the world. If an important task of the intervenor is to provide a presence otherwise lacking in a system, it follows that an effective intervenor should be able to move from one presence to another. This is an ideal that at best can only be approximated by most practitioners. While one can learn to be explicit at some moments and mysterious at others, the power of presence comes from coherence and deep internalization of basic values and visions, something that can only be achieved over many years of self-development. To "role play" would be disastrous and would defeat the purpose and impact of modeling. Three conclusions offer a way out of this dilemma:

1. The sense of feeling at home and "right" about being in the role of intervenor in itself conveys great power, regardless of stylistic variations or differences in theory of how to teach.
2. Since many organizations have greater difficulty at the awareness level than at other points of the Cycle of Experience, any presence that models the importance of being aware of process will have a significant impact.
3. No single intervenor can give a system all that it needs. For optimal organization learning, numerous presences that model different theories of learning may be required. This may well be an argument calling for multiple presences in any system intervention.

REFERENCES

Adelson, J. "The teacher as model." *The American Scholar*, vol. 30, no. 3 (Summer, 1961), 383–406.

Buber, M. *Tales of the Hasidim: The Early Masters.* New York: Schocken Books, 1947, 1975.

Flax, S. "Can Chrysler keep rolling along?" Jan. 7, 1985, 34–39.

Kopp, S. *Guru, Metaphors From a Psychotherapist.* Palo Alto, Calif.: Science and Behavior Books, 1971.

Kopp, S. *If You Meet the Buddha on the Road, Kill Him!* Palo Alto, Calif.: Science and Behavior Books, 1972.

Legge, J. (trans.). *The Philosophy of Confucius.* New York: Crescent Books, undated.

Unidentified author. *Buddha: His Life and Times.* New York: Crescent Books, 1974.

Weisel, E. *Souls on Fire.* New York: Vintage Books, 1973.

Yalom, I, Lieberman, B., and Miles, M. *Encounter Groups: First Facts.* New York: Basic Books, 1973.

5
The Desired Skills of a Competent Intervenor

> Lives can be profoundly affected or even lost because of the way information is conveyed. Admittedly, patients vary in their ability to live with the truth, and sometimes the truth can complicate and impair treatment. Truth, misplaced or poorly conveyed, can crush two vital ingredients in treatment—hope and the will to live. Since everyone in this post-Watergate world wants to avoid the stigma attached to lying, I feel compelled to say that the issue here is not *whether* to tell the truth but *how* to tell the truth. Dr. Oliver Wendell Holmes summed it up when he told his medical students that successful medical practice requires not lying but an ability by a physician to "round the sharp corners of truth." Truth can be told in a way that can potentiate a patient or devastate him. It can lead to challenge or set the stage for shattering defeat.
>
> Norman Cousins, *The Healing Heart,* (1983).

One of the qualities that distinguishes skilled professionals from novices or nonprofessional persons is the depth and breadth of their awareness in the area of their specialty. The range of stimuli that is responded to, and that leads to formation of figures of interest, is significantly greater for the experienced professional. In fact, the training of the professional is basically designed to enhance this awareness. An important feature of the teaching of professionals in any field is that the student learn about, and broaden, awareness.

One aspect of this awareness is that the skilled person knows what questions to ask himself or herself in the pursuit of professional work. These questions concern what is needed at each step of the process.

- Are data needed for diagnostic or problem-identification purposes?
- Do I have sufficient awareness of what is going on within the client and within myself?
- What is the readiness for a given intervention on my part?
- Is there sufficient energy in the client system to do the work required if growth is to occur?
- What is the nature of my relationship with the client? Is it conducive to movement by the client?
- What is the best thing for me to do at this moment in order to be helpful?

The deeper and wider the awareness of the professional, the greater and more varied the questions that may be self-addressed. Whether this questioning process is explicit or intuitive and nonarticulated, all skilled practitioners engage in it as they carry out their practice. In *The Reflective Practitioner,* Donald Schon (1983) looks at this process as it unfolds in cases drawn from five professions. He calls the process "reflection in action," focusing on how professionals think while they act. While this work makes a fine contribution to our understanding of professional practice, Schon does not explain the content of the practitioner's awareness before the action but is concerned mainly with the nature of the thought process behind the questioning.

A Gestalt approach focuses more on the awareness that precedes self-questioning, and on the specific behavioral repertoire that one may work from in response to the answers to the questions. The emphasis is on the skills of awareness and action rather than on the questions, although Gestalt awareness process may be seen as a form of self-questioning. Thus when the skills of attending or observing are employed, the consultant is engaged in an ongoing attempt to take in data that will help in answering one or more questions of the kind mentioned above. One cannot operate effectively without self-questioning; all approaches to professional practice make this clear. The special feature of Gestalt-oriented training is that it stresses the development of heightened awareness which helps to inform or direct the nature of the questioning. In addition, as the use of self (presence) is central to Gestalt practice, the skills of sharing, of supporting mobilization of energy (joining), and of facilitating contact, are emphasized. The remainder of this chapter enumerates and discusses a large number of specific skills that distinguish a competent consultant.

The skills required to be effective in using a Gestalt approach follow from the use of the Cycle of Experience as an orientation for client and self. While the phenomena involved are often hard to operationalize in specific terms, it is important to try to identify concrete, specific behaviors that form the basis for client and consultant effectiveness. By modeling these behaviors personally, the consultant enhances the learning of the client system. Beginning with the work of Fritz Perls, classical Gestalt methodology has stressed work at the microscopic behavior levels of awareness and contact. Indeed, one criterion of effective client development in dealing with troublesome issues has long been that of movement to specific actions or statements from initial periods of vagueness, confusion, overgeneralization, and the like. This point is discussed in most basic books, such as Polster and Polster (1973), as well as Kepner and Brien (1970), who refer to the approach as "behavioristic phenomenology." These authors consider phenomenological events to be actual behaviors.

This perspective does not imply that any interesting or striking behavior is potentially useful, as might seem true by the tendency of unskilled practitioners to assume that congruent personal style is the goal and that one is effective by being "authentic" or "who I am." Rather, the perspective attempts to stay true to those actions that further the system learning process implied by the Cycle of Experience. From this standpoint the issue becomes more one of tactical choice: What behavior is useful at a particular moment? The skills presented herein form a repertoire of possible or available behaviors from which the intervenor may draw. These are the behaviors that enable new awareness to develop in the client system in such a way that it can be taken in and digested.

In Chapter 3, five basic activities of a Gestalt-oriented consultant were outlined.

1. To attend to the client system, observe, and selectively share observations of what you see, hear, etc., establishing your presence in doing so.

2. To attend to your own experience (feelings, sensations, thoughts) and selectively share these, establishing your presence in doing so.

3. To focus on energy in the client system and the emergence of or lack of issues (common figures) for which there is energy; to act to support mobilization of energy (joining) so that something happens.

4. To facilitate clear, meaningful, heightened contacts between members of the client system (including contact with you).

5. To help the group achieve heightened awareness of its process in completing units of work, and to learn how to complete units of work so as to achieve closure around problem areas and unfinished business.

The behavioral skills presented below relate to these basic tasks and serve to actualize observation, sharing, energy mobilization, contact enhancement, and so forth.* They are grouped in terms of the major task they highlight, such as attending or sharing, though many of the categories are useful for more than one activity. In reviewing this list it is imperative to keep in mind that these skills refer both to behavior of the consultant and the skills that are critical for improved client functioning. The consultant employs these to achieve client movement on the problems at hand, and is a teacher to the system of these very same skills.

REQUIRED BEHAVIORAL SKILLS*

Skills Related to Observation, Attending, Taking in the Raw Data of Experience

In this category are those actions and attitudes that enhance awareness. It is through these behaviors that one comes to know what is going on in others and in self. For this reason we may think of them as building blocks or positioning skills, those actions from which all else follows. Since this is a "taking-in" phase, many of the behaviors listed are designed to enhance the

* A shorter list was first developed about ten years ago by C. Wesley Jackson, a senior faculty member of the Gestalt Institute of Cleveland, as an attempt to state behavioral objectives in the teaching of helping professionals. I am greatly indebted to him for the stimulation provided by his work.

openness and sensitivity of the consultant as compared with more assertive, motorically related skills. Some of the following skills derive from values and attitudes, and are displayed in a very subtle manner. They are learned behaviors that have to do mainly with a belief that patience and minimal response is often very useful.

A. Ability to Stay in the Present and to Focus on the Ongoing Process, with Faith in Natural Developmental Sequences

1. Having ability to be patient and receptive in dealings with clients, particularly in early stages of a given piece of work.
2. Having ability to tolerate confusion and ambiguity without rushing to organize.
3. Having little need to make powerful things happen or to force action.
4. Accepting responsibility for and respecting own feelings of frustration, boredom, unmet expectations.
5. Having ability to trust the strength and potential availability of seemingly unavailable people (e.g., those least active or positive in response to your intervention).
6. Being aware of deflective behavior in self or others (distracting behavior, changing of topic, telling "war stories," etc.).
7. Appreciating that an unfinished situation, long-standing problem, or conflict is not dealt with easily; tolerance for the working-through process in systems of any kind or size.
8. Avoiding of "gimmicks" to speed things up.
9. Being able to tell the difference between the various stages of the Cycle of Experience and to support client attention to a given level without hurrying to the next stage.
10. Having faith in the inherent desire of any living system to function well and to be healthy; recognition that destructive systems are responsible for the state of their affairs.
11. Accepting your task as that of education, not salvation; ability to work from a posture of "creative indifference."

B. Considerable Sensitivity to Sensory, Physical Functioning of Self and Others

1. Having ability to stay open to experience: can see, hear, touch, taste, etc., with ease and without straining or thinking.

2. Having good sensory discrimination; can see and use a range of stimuli and can appreciate variations in intensity of experiences.

3. Being aware of own sensory blindspots or underdeveloped faculties (e.g., are you better at seeing than at hearing?).

4. Having the ability to sense and track how others use their senses; can tell when someone appears to be desensitized or is denying sensory input.

5. Accepting body functioning; being comfortable with own body.

6. Being aware of, sensitive to, a range of gestures, postures, movements in self and others.

7. Having ability to separate voice qualities from word content, and to identify a range of qualities (e.g., tone, pitch, emotion).

8. Being aware of tension indicators; of one or more individuals tightening their musculature or otherwise "holding back."

9. Understanding of the quality of good breathing and body centering; awareness of importance of breathing for support of self or others.

10. At the group system level, having the ability to track interactional patterns of talking, listening, touching, etc.; awareness of what people want from each other.

11. Having ability to hear, see, intuit what people are asking or expecting of you at a given moment.

C. Frequent Tuning Into Your Emotional Reactions and Those of Others

1. Having good contact with emotions; can experience different emotions in self and others.

2. Having a wide range of feelings available to you; can make discriminations in quality and intensity.

3. Being aware of your emotional blindspots, underdeveloped emotions, or denial areas.

4. Being able to tell the difference between confrontation through direct expression of strong feelings and the use of teasing, sarcasm, ridicule, etc., as an avoidance of true feelings.

5. Having ability to recognize complex emotional patterns in small systems or groups; can appreciate the interactional aspects of moods, emotional states, etc.

6. Appreciating the relationship between depression and blocked aggression.

Skills Related to the Sharing of Experience by the Consultant

This category includes those behaviors through which experience is articulated and communicated to others. These are the actions that follow from awareness and that build on the raw data of observation of self and other. Moreover, these actions become additional sources of awareness for both client and consultant. When put forth well—with focus, clarity, and good timing—the client's awareness is stimulated. The consultant gets to hear and feel what it is like to share his or her internal experience, to say what may be only partially formulated before the action is attempted. These are the behaviors of movement from a receptive stance to greater engagement with the client system, but which do not have the full force required for intense contact.

D. Ability to Separate Data from Interpretation and to Emphasize Nonjudgmental Observations

1. Having ability to stay as close as possible to raw, immediate data in both observation and articulation of what is observed.
2. Having ability to comment on events in a nonjudgmental manner.
3. Being able to distinguish between "descriptive" and "evaluative" observations in self, and for others.
4. Having ability to express tentatively held views, as opposed to dogmatic certainties.
5. Understanding of the assumptions or biases from which you operate.
6. Having ability to make interesting statements that imply or allow for more than one interpretation of an observed event; to provide several "hypotheses" for the client.
7. Having ability to use formulations or conjectures about the motivation of others as orienting hypotheses for oneself, rather than as statements of "truth" to be shared; offering such statements only when the client seems sincerely interested in hearing them.

E. Ability to Put Things Succinctly, Clearly, and Directly

1. Having ability to use crisp, clean language.
2. Being easily understood by others.

3. Usage of metaphor, simile, and other poetic forms; use of color and force in phrasing.
4. Maintaining congruency of word, body movement, gestures.
5. Being brief and concise, knowing how to be short and pithy.
6. Keeping remarks on topic.
7. Having available a wide variety of references to places, names, things, and personal experiences, and using these to widen the perspective or context of your remarks.
8. Possessing skill in articulating difficult or painful observations, feelings, or insights; ability to "speak the unspeakable" in a graceful, direct, yet nonattacking way.

F. Awareness of Your Intentions, of What You Want to Do or Say, Together with the Ability to be Clear in Letting Others Know What You Want of and From Them

1. Being clear when asking others to do something, or in posing questions.
2. Having ability to state observations so that clients can use them; can state problems clearly.
3. Having sense of focus on what you are doing, even when you are confused or uncertain.
4. Having ability to be specific in posing experiments to clients; setting tasks that are clear and manageable.
5. Having ability to target and reach the core of a problem; can add to client's articulation of theme or problem by giving clear, supportive direction for next steps.
6. Understanding congruence of what you feel or perceive and how this is communicated to client.
7. Having ability to pose dilemmas in a way that leads to "useful frustration" on part of client.

Skills Related to the Mobilization and Modulation of Client System Energy

This category includes both attitudinal sets and more overt behavioral manifestations. These skills are companions to those of sharing, as they are carried out according to the manner in which the consultant advances or holds back his or her energy and excitement. Some of the skills are clearly those of containment or bracketing of the consultant's experience, enabling the client's process to continue with little or no interference by the consultant. Others have to do with more active intervention in the process. In any event, all of these skills deal with the management of energy in the system. If energy is mobilizing well, there is less to intervene about. If it appears that the system is not capable of handling the force of energy being mobilized, or if the system is acting out of limited awareness or pseudojoining, the consultant may wish to become more active in helping to slow things down for examination or better pacing.

G. Ability to See Where Client is at Any Time, and to Respect That in Working with the System

1. Being sensitive to issues of timing; can hold back or wait to make observations.
2. Having ability to allow client system process to emerge according to its nature; to stay grounded in a system that is not well known to you.
3. Being able to hold own needs in abeyance in order to move with others.
4. Having ability to build on awareness, tensions, energy of client, by adding your own interest and energy.
5. Having ability to be patient yet active in heightening client resistance.
6. Having ability to remain at an awareness level if client is not ready to move ahead.
7. Having sensitivity to and ability to pace or stretch others incrementally and in manageable steps, avoiding attempts at "instant solutions."
8. Not seeing resistant clients as "enemies to be overcome;" nonbullying and noncompetitive with clients.
9. Having ability to modulate, monitor, perhaps stop interactions among client system members in order to prevent nonfunctional contacts or premature closure.

H. Ability to Face and Accept Emotional Situations with a Minimum of Personal Defensiveness

1. Having ability to face conflict, anger.
2. Having ability to tolerate and accept closeness, affection.
3. Having ability to stand silence.
4. Having ability to tolerate tension.

5. Having ability to know when to contain or defuse, versus heightening and expanding, emotional situations.

6. Knowing how to uphold the rights of individuals to resist group pressures if they so choose.

7. Tolerating criticism of self without becoming aggressive in response; staying with own "resistance," or vulnerability.

8. Remaining in contact with client even though personally upset or anxious; can "bracket" own feelings for later attention.

9. Being able to allow interpersonal conflict to emerge openly and to support it without rushing in to stop it too soon, or to wait too long and allow it to get out of hand.

10. Having ability to recognize and cope with people who are developing, or have developed, more stress than they can handle or who are in danger of being seriously embarrassed in front of others.

Skills Related to the Enhancement of Contact

These are the behaviors that promote engagement to the point at which people attend to and interact with each other in a highly involving way. The behaviors are very closely related to, and overlap with, those used in the mobilization and modulation of energy. As with the management of energy, the consultant acts to enhance contact when it appears to be developing. By presenting a very appealing manner, the consultant motivates the client to make contact. The strength of this appeal acts as a "grabber," so that the client is interested in what the consultant has to offer. However, if it is too strong, it may interfere with the consultant's attempts to enhance contact among the members of the client system. Also, as with the management of energy, there will be times when the consultant will act to slow down or modulate contact. This is particularly important when the members of the client system differ in the kind of contact they wish to have at a given moment.

I. Ability to Make Good Contact With Others

1. Having capacity to become interested in a wide range of human behavior.

2. Being able to be at ease when others want to move close to you or want to know you better; are available without being unnecessarily revealing.

3. Having appreciation of the usefulness of sharing your feelings and fantasies.

4. Having appreciation of the difference between asking questions and making statements.

5. Understanding and respecting your particular rhythm or need for contact with others and need for contact with self.

6. Knowing the language of emotion; having a varied vocabulary with which to express discriminations in experience (e.g., difference between sadness and depression).

7. Having ability to express your feelings authentically rather than as a "gimmick."

8. Having ability to know when expressing your feelings is not functional; can hold back when necessary and avoid disruptive openness.

J. Ability to Present Self as a Highly Attractive Yet Noncharismatic Presence

1. Making sure own individuality is clear but not overly dominating.

2. Exhibiting relatively little projection of your needs upon others, yet being "up front" about your values and what you are teaching.

3. Being able to share own experiences in a useful, nondisruptive way.

4. Allowing room for others to influence what happens without abdicating your leadership.

5. Being personally "there," but not a "buddy" to clients.

6. Making creative, innovative aspects of your life-style known to clients, but not selling them as "the way."

7. Having ability to get others interested in attending to or being with you without fostering their dependency upon you.

8. Showing graciousness with clients; having little need to flaunt your accomplishments or skills, and being generous in sharing with others.

9. Showing a strong personality, but having nonthreatening way of relating to others.

K. Capacity to be Both Tough and Supportive During the Same Work Session

1. Being aware that confrontation means firm, direct contact, not aggression or love.

2. Being able to share strong feelings or thoughts in a straight, forceful, yet caring way.

3. Having ability to disagree openly with client without being contentious or disruptive.

4. Being able to express warm feelings without being "gushy."

5. Being able to express praise, recognition, or appreciation for what others have done without use of flattery.

6. Being able to express disappointment in client behavior without being punitive.

7. Being able to touch people physically or verbally when it is truly helpful; being able to know when to refrain from doing so.

8. Being able to push people hard without being "bought off" by their fragility.

9. Having ability to articulate painful observations about the client and then to be generous in support of client follow-through in responding.

Skills Related to Closure and the Completion of Units of Work

This category includes behaviors that articulate the educational nature of the work and that focus on the meaning of the experience of each aspect of the work or of the intervention as a whole. It also embraces those actions or attitudes that acknowledge or take into account the context within which the work is performed. While the behaviors employed in sharing and enhancement of contact are useful in this phase of the work, at this point the consultant's task is to respond to the diminishing energy that occurs when the work is finished, and also to help the system to recognize what has not been accomplished or completed. Summarization of what took place, generalization or application of the learning, and plans or steps for future work are the issues that these behaviors address.

L. Ability to Help the Client System Draw Meaning or Understanding From Its Experience With the Consultant

1. Having ability to design interventions that deal with manageable issues so that a sense of accomplishment is possible for the client.

2. Having good sense of timing with regard to what can be accomplished within a given period of work.

3. Being aware of what stage of the Cycle of Experience is the most fruitful to address at a given time.

4. Appreciating the importance of withdrawal of energy after work has been done; recognizing the need for assimilation of an experience before moving on to another.

5. Being able to close each period of contact with the client in such a way that the system has some next step clearly in mind, or some specific skill to use or practice.

6. Having ability to help clients draw meaning from their experience, no matter what it is; knowing how to support time and effort for "cognitive capping."

7. Having ability to be didactic at appropriate moments; being able to expose client system to content enrichment materials or broader value perspectives without interrupting the client's process of learning.

M. Appreciation of the Significant Contextual Issues Involved in System Interventions

1. Being clear in own mind that your role is to use process interventions in the support of improvement of the system's way of carrying out its work.

2. Knowing stages of development of different kinds of systems, and being able to relate interventions to system maturity.

3. Being aware of and considering the possible consequences at other levels when making an intervention at any given level or part of that system.

4. Being aware of own skills, strengths, and limitations with regard to the nature of the problem or client and the use of various techniques or methodologies of system consulting.

5. Appreciating the dynamic quality of intervention in an ongoing social system; continual awareness of the changing nature of the client and the contract.

6. Having ability to remain in a marginal role and to keep boundary issues in mind as the work progresses; being able to achieve a functional balance between high acceptance by the client and nonconfluent attachment.

Skills Related to Appreciation of Consultation as the Practice of an Art

The behaviors in this category do not follow strictly from a Gestalt perspective. They are valid for all approaches to changing social systems. However, they are particularly relevant to the Gestalt framework because they fit well within a phenomenological point of view. The items acknowledge that reality cannot be grasped simply from linear, rational thinking, and also that there is something of the absurd in thinking that one can truly influence a social system. Finally, this category emphasizes the creative nature of the work.

N. Awareness of the Aesthetic, Transcendent, and Creative Aspects of Working as a Consultant

1. Possessing some sense of awe about the undertaking.
2. Having a strong sense of curiosity or playfulness about life happenings.
3. Having ability to use irony, paradox, enigma, and humor.
4. Appreciating the importance of fantasy and imagination.
5. Having ability to integrate some sense of mysticism with a cognitive, rational approach.
6. Being able to appreciate and use references or examples from art, music, theater, technology, etc.
7. Having ability to reach for and use a wide range of options.
8. Being open to potentialities; an eclectic outlook rather than being partisan, dogmatic.
9. Being able to appreciate both a sense of power and of humility in what you are trying to do.

DEVELOPMENT AND USE OF SKILLS

Upon reviewing these behaviors and attitudes, some questions should be considered.

- Are these personality traits or are they abilities?
- How are these qualities or skills acquired?
- Are some of these attributes more important than others?
- Are there any guidelines or criteria that can direct the consultant's choice among these behaviors?

These questions are difficult to answer. However, some comments may be useful in this regard. To be able to display any or all of these qualities there is no substitute for an almost innate curiosity about the raw data of human experience, one's own, as well as that of others. Obviously the developmental histories of consultants will result in a variety of sensitivities and predispositions for acting in the ways indicated above. One who has developed a strong interest in observing self and other, and who has turned this into a career as a helping professional, will have a foundation upon which to build.

More important than whether one has the appropriate personality is whether one can acknowledge the need to learn these skills, to practice them, and to receive feedback as to one's performance. An individual may have some inborn musical aptitude but years of study and practice are required to become an accomplished musician; the same is true of becoming an accomplished consultant of any persuasion. In the Gestalt perspective, the major area of study and practice involves the use of self as an instrument. One must develop exceptionally acute powers of observation and articulation to be effective in using this approach. The skills can be learned if one is willing to pay the price in time and effort. Numerous effective consultants who work from other perspectives possess great skill in many of the areas listed above—skill developed out of their interest and experience in observing and understanding.

There are two ways in which these skills can be developed. The first has to do with personal development. Learning to be aware, to be able to position oneself in the world so that all kinds of experience can be taken in and appreciated, is aided immensely by participation in various personal growth programs, including psychotherapy, encounter groups, meditation, and body process programs such as Feldenkrais and the Alexander Technique. In addition, many people have found that some training in art, music, theater, or dance has been of great benefit in the development of the skills of attending and sharing, as well as for an appreciation of the importance of presence in general.

The second arena for development of these skills is that of practice in settings that allow for feedback. There is no substitute for practical experiences that provide for experimentation combined with some kind of feedback mechanism. This may take place in a formal training program or in on-the-job consultation with a partner who can provide good feedback concerning the use of concepts and specific behavior. One of the most powerful formats of this kind is to have two people work as consultants, but one as a consultant to the other, who serves as the consultant to the system. The observer-feedback consultant talks only to the working consultant during the actual contact with the client. The aim is to keep the working consultant constantly aware of what he or she is doing, and to highlight the assumptions from which this behavior follows. This arrangement is better suited to a training or internship setting than to one where a great deal of experience is required. However, when applied in both settings, it has proven valuable for clients to hear the consultant "talk out loud" about many things that are not usually made explicit. It increases consultant sharing and tends to enlarge client awareness.

The presentation of this list of attributes does not provide a guideline for choosing a particular stance or behavior at any given moment, but rather, a repertoire from which to choose. Some guidance in this respect is implied in the skills for *"Ability to Stay in the Present" (category A),* and *"Ability to See Where the Client is at Any Time" (category G).* By being able to stay rooted in the present moment, and to remain in the here-and-now, the consultant is in touch with the situation and can behave accordingly. This will not always prove to be effective, but if the behavior has any impact on the client, the consultant will soon find out that something else is needed. It is also important to realize that some of the behaviors enumerated may never be used with certain clients, or will be used infrequently. Most organizational settings have strong norms controlling the expression of feelings, fantasies, and other personal experiences. The mark of an astute practitioner is the ability to be aware of this and to move appropriately in dealing with such boundaries.

It should also be acknowledged that this is not an exhaustive list and that many other items might be added. In particular, items dealing with the use of techniques and with design of system interventions are barely covered.* The skills discussed refer to how the consultant acts in doing a variety of things that make up the actual work of a consulting assignment. The em-

---

* For discussion of the technology of organization consulting from a process perspective, the reader is referred to books by Burke (1982), Beckhard (1969), Beckhard and Harris (1977), Levinson (1972), Dyer (1977), Nadler (1977), Schein (1969), and Weisbord (1978).

phasis is mainly on how one uses oneself to model the processes of the Cycle of Experience and to enhance movement by the client system in dealing with its problems. Armed with the ability to employ these actions, the consultant is ready to use methods and techniques with a high degree of effectiveness.

REFERENCES

Beckhard, R. *Organization Development: Strategies and Models.* Reading, Mass.: Addison-Wesley, 1969.

Beckhard, R., and Harris, R. *Organizational Transitions: Managing Complex Change.* Reading, Mass.: Addison-Wesley, 1977.

Burke, W.W. *Organization Development.* Boston: Little, Brown, 1982.

Cousins, N. *The Healing Heart.* New York: Norton, 1983.

Dyer, W.G. *Team Building.* Reading, Mass.: Addison-Wesley, 1977.

Kepner, E., and Brien, L. "Gestalt therapy: A behavioristic phenomenology." in J. Fagan, and I.E. Sheperd, (eds.), *Gestalt Therapy Now.* Palo Alto, Calif.: Science and Behavior Books, 1970.

Levinson, H. *Organization Diagnosis.* Cambridge, Mass.: Harvard University Press, 1972.

Nadler, D.A. *Feedback and Organization Development: Using Data-Based Methods.* Reading, Mass.: Addison-Wesley, 1977.

Polster, E., and Polster, M. *Gestalt Therapy Integrated.* New York: Brunner/Mazel, 1973.

Schein, E.H. *Process Consultation.* Reading, Mass.: Addison-Wesley, 1969.

Schon, D.A. *The Reflective Practitioner.* New York: Basic Books, 1983.

Weisbord, M.A. *Organizational Diagnosis.* Reading, Mass.: Addison-Wesley, 1978.

6
Gestalt Awareness Process in Organizational Assessment

The main thesis of this chapter is that an understanding of Gestalt awareness process changes the nature of assessment, enhances the richness of the data gathered in diagnostic work, and leads to intervention behaviors that allow for high consultant impact and acceptance. Gestalt awareness process can be added to current models for organizational diagnosis in such a way as to broaden rather than diminish the usefulness of other analytical methods. The result is an integrative action model that allows for use of the full self of the consultant in the assessment process.*

The leading practitioners of organization development place great emphasis on proper diagnosis as the cornerstone of their approach, and have developed important models and methods for gathering data and determining points of organizational dysfunction, need for change, and appropriate entry points and strategies. Beckhard (1974, 1977), one of the first to see clearly the need for a change model resting solidly on diagnosis, has developed a very useful and durable scheme for looking at a sys-

*Since "diagnosis" implies illness and cause–effect relationships, and "assessment" is an estimate of the importance or value of things, I prefer the latter term to signify the "sizing up" of a system by a consultant. I will continue to use diagnostic terminology in order to be consistent with the fact that almost all practitioners use the term "diagnosis."

tem and doing effective change planning. Levinson (1972) has developed a highly detailed outline for what he calls an "organization examination," one that holds significant consultant recommendation until an exhaustive data-gathering phase has been conducted. Likewise, Nadler (1974), Mahler (1974), and others have emphasized data-based interventions and ways of putting diagnostic findings before the client as an important part of the consulting relationship. These procedures generally follow the research model of the pioneering work in the study of organizations by Likert and his associates at the Institute for Social Research (1961). Weisbord's "six-Box model" (1976, 1978) is similar, but is designed so that the consultation process can begin sooner; diagnosis is used to find sources of energy for work to take place.

To appreciate fully the perspective of these attempts to study organizations, it will be useful to look at the aim and definition of diagnosis. According to Levinson (1972), the aim is to examine an organization in order to assess its well-being and to decide what, if anything, needs to be done to help. His model is clearly borrowed from a medical-psychiatric approach and rests upon the study of illness and dysfunction:

> The most highly systematized examinational procedure for a living system is that used for the physical and psychatric examination of the individual. . . . the extrapolation seemed to me even more appropriate, for my whole effort to learn more about mental health in industry was from a clinical, specifically psychoanalytic, point of view. (p.X)

This model is consistent with the definition of diagnosis as a means by which to decide the nature of a diseased condition, and it is consistent with a deterministically oriented, scientific approach to the understanding, explaining, and predicting of behavior. It is a search for the *right* thing to do, supported by the implication that cause and effect can be determined, and that other actions will be *wrong* if the diagnosis is correct. Furthermore, the traditional diagnostic model rises or falls on the expertise of the consultant; she or he must somehow assertively search out the important data and make the correct deductions (interpretations?) from the data gathered in the diagnostic work-up. This is, of course, the classical medical model, and is the basis for what Schein (1969, 1977) has called the "doctor–patient" consultation model.

DIAGNOSIS AS HYPOTHESIS FORMATION

A more flexible way to view diagnosis is to consider it as hypothesis formation. This perspective implies that complex illnesses or organization problems do not readily lend themselves to simple cause–effect analysis, and that the data needed to understand these problems can only be obtained through immersion in them over a period of time. In this approach the consultant does successive approximations of an understanding of a problem, gathering data leading to an hypothesis that informs some kind of "treatment," using data gathered during this treatment phase to derive a later hypothesis, and so on. Thus an action based on a diagnosis may not lead to a solution, and another search is made to find what was missed. This process is no different from that of any researcher who does numerous experiments on the road to a discovery. What makes the situation more complicated when dealing with problems of a social system is that an enormous amount of data or awareness is potentially available for study. The consultant must make choices as to what figures to develop out of a complex background.

If we think of diagnosis as a process of hypothesis formation, it is important to understand what is an effective balance between an uninterrupted, unbiased flow of awareness and translation of the data of awareness into workable hypotheses. The consultant's dilemma is that both are necessary but balance must be achieved in the midst of live, dynamic situations, including issues of time, access to organization, and contract restraints.

To understand the process of hypothesis formation better, we can contrast two approaches that may be seen as opposites or extremes. The first approach stresses gathering of observable external data and the building of deductions from critical incidents. This method places value on the ability of the observer to make useful connections as soon as possible; the faster an hypothesis can be generated, the better. The skillful practitioner can take limited data and, adding analytical reasoning ability and the wisdom of experience, generate a workable hypothesis fairly quickly. An underlying assumption here is that useful data do emerge early, and that even limited awareness or knowledge can lead to useful solutions when provided to an expert. The linear, sequential mode of this approach may be a manifestation of left-brain functioning, as this mode of consciousness has been described by Ornstein (1977) and others.

I refer to this approach as the "Sherlock Holmes Model."* As master detective, Sherlock Holmes epitomizes the analytic, scientific model that emerged at the end of the 19th century. Consider these quotations of Holmes from the Baring-Gould (1967) annotation of the A. Conan Doyle stories:

> The ideal reasoner . . . would, when he had been shown a single fact in all its bearings, deduce from it not only the chain of events which lead up to it, but also all the results which would follow from it. As Couvier could correctly describe a whole animal from the contemplation of a single bone, so the observer who has thoroughly understood one link in a series of incidents should be able to accurately state all the other ones, both before and after.
>
> "Data, data, data," he cried impatiently. "I can't make bricks without clay."
>
> It is of the first importance . . . not to allow your judgement to be biased by personal qualities. A client to me is a mere unit, a factor in a problem. The emotional qualities are antagonistic to clear reasoning.
>
> I do not waste words or disclose my thoughts while a case is actually under consideration.
>
> I claim the right to work in my own way and give my results at my own time—complete, rather than in stages.

*Marcello Truzzi's paper on "Sherlock Holmes as Applied Social Scientist" (1976) helped me to see this analogy.

DIRECTED VERSUS UNDIRECTED AWARENESS

Sherlock Holmes does not make wild speculations based on sparse data; he is an acute, careful observer. He said: "It is a capital mistake to theorize before you have all the data" (Baring-Gould, 1967). However, the key factor for Holmes is his ability to do deductive reasoning, to use the power of his mind to draw the right conclusion from limited information. Holmes takes this limited information and develops the remainder of the story in his mind. He uses his mind to force additional data to emerge and make sense. In the language of Gestalt therapy, this is referred to as the process of *active, directed awareness*. Since this approach rests a great deal upon expertise and confidence in making inferences, its practitioners rely heavily on logic and analytical reasoning. Along with this is the belief that a few critical facts may lead to the proper conclusion, and that the quicker this is done, the better.

A second process of hypothesis formation may be contrasted with this model. This process relies on *open, undirected awareness*. It is based on the contention that one cannot force data to emerge, and that one must become immersed in a setting and wait until it emerges. There is no less emphasis on powers of observation than in the first process, but there is an assumption that the observer does not know where to direct attention until more information is available. As in Schein's (1977) point about the value of process consultation, the assumption is that the important data are embedded in the system and not readily available to anyone at first. Thus this is an unfocused approach that tends to treat everything as equal and to hold back in forming figures of interest. Information is processed more diffusely and an attempt is made to enlarge inputs until some integration is possible. It may well be that this is an aspect of right-brain functioning (see Ornstein, 1977, p. 21).

If Sherlock Holmes is a metaphor for the directed awareness approach, a metaphor for the undirected mode is Detective Columbo, hero of the TV series. Unlike Holmes, who is well-organized, precise, knowing, superior in perception and logical reasoning, rational and deductively oriented, Columbo is naive, rambling, slow moving, seemingly unfocused in his perceptiveness, and fuzzy, if not downright illogical. He is disheveled in appearance (rather than trim and neat like Holmes), does not appear to be working from a predetermined specific guideline of significant variables to check, nor does he seem to know where he is going from one moment to the next. While Holmes is never seen making a misstep—unless momentarily outwitted by a superior mind (Dr. Moriarty, for example)—Columbo seems to be faltering or bumbling most of the time.

Columbo may be said to act like a sponge, immersing himself in his milieu and waiting for important clues to be drawn to him. Holmes resembles a finely trained hunting dog who attacks his settings, and he never rests until he has put the pieces together in his mind. Columbo teaches or coaxes the people and environment involved to "give up" data as he makes contact with them. Holmes educates himself by being in *control* of his environment; Columbo *allows* himself to be educated. Holmes rarely makes close, personal contact with the villain; Columbo's method rests largely upon repeated personal contacts. One of the trademarks of a Columbo case is the expressed irritation of the villain at being asked the same question many times, or at being asked by Columbo for permission to wander around settings he has already traversed more than once.

The reader who is knowledgeable in the philosophy of science will recognize that the Holmes approach is an application of 19th-century science as it combined technical discoveries with logical analysis. The method of Columbo is an application of 20th-century existentialism and its emphasis upon uncertainty, being, and here-and-now phenomena.

GESTALT AWARENESS PROCESS

Gestalt awareness process recognizes the value of both directed and undirected awareness. These approaches are described in Table 6-1. As seen from this table, *active, directed*

Table 6-1. Gestalt Awareness Process

Active, Directed Awareness	*Open, Undirected Awareness*
Goes to the world	Lets the world come to you
Forces something to emerge	Waits for something to emerge
Uses a structure/framework to guide what you wish to see, hear, etc.	Investigates without being organized or "prejudiced" in any way as to what you wish to see, hear, etc.
Focuses questioning; strives for a narrow, sharp field of vision	Maintains widest peripheral vision; little foreground and everything of equal importance
Attends to things in terms of knowledge of how they work, what is present and missing in a normative sense	Is naive about how things work; hopes to find something new about how things work
Searching use of sensory modalities	Receptive use of sensory modalities
Supports work by content values and conceptual biases	Values are process-oriented, tend to be content-free

awareness describes the procedures most often used by organization development consultants and action research practitioners, emphasizing structured, guided questioning of members of the client system. The Gestalt-oriented consultant uses these procedures but also places heavy emphasis on *open, undirected awareness* and attempts to hold hypothesis formation in abeyance for a longer period of time. (It should be noted, in this respect, that any system or model that is based on predetermined areas for organizational study implies that one has hypotheses about what is important to study before even beginning the study). Open, undirected awareness is an attempt to reduce bias and to remain as naive as possible while engaged in diagnosis.

If we can appreciate the utility of the open/Columbo approach, we need to ask why this method has been underutilized by organizational consultants up to this point. Why is it that spongelike absorption is seen as secondary in importance to directed awareness? It would appear that the scientific/medical model has been adopted by many as the appropriate paradigm for organizational diagnosis. Many of the foremost early practitioners were either trained in or influenced by this model, and view diagnosis as an application of its research methods. An important aspect of this model is that of impersonality and rationality in making observations. This has been bolstered by the very fact that years of research and consultation have yielded much by way of concepts and data as to how organizations work or do not work well. The practitioner who is aware of this body of knowledge need not start from a blank page each time. The directed awareness approach takes this knowledge into consideration, so that informed hypotheses may speed up the work of diagnosis. Finally, for many practitioners, diagnosis is considered an intellectual problem or challenge, not an opportunity to engage in or become involved with the client system. Even the participant-observation methods of ethnomethodologists, who immerse themselves for long periods of time in a cultural milieu, are designed to study the culture but not to enhance interventions.

Of interest, in this regard, is the work of Levinson (1972). His approach to organizational diagnosis is possibly the most thorough developed to date. Not only is his case study outline complete, but the method is such that many months are required to gather the data for diagnosis. Moreover, he insists upon doing this work before providing a diagnosis and recommendations to the client. To his credit he holds firm to his value that one should not force data or act on limited or incomplete information. While others have developed similar diagnostic guides, Levinson's rests on a strong theoretical foundation—that of psychoanalysis—and may be as good a method of active, directed, awareness as can be found anywhere. The method allows for open, undirected awareness, and Levinson contends that some unfocused wandering around should be done by the consultant. (Indeed, it is improbable that any good observer will spend six or eight months gathering information in an organization without picking up, serendipitously, highly useful data not called for in a case study outline.) Unfortunately, Levinson's method tends to downplay how the consultant can use himself or herself more, and how intuitiveness can aid in the interpretation of the enormous amount of information gathered. By adding the kinds of data made possible by a more receptive approach, and by enlarging the concept of data to be more akin to that of awareness (as awareness is defined in Chapter 2), his method would be enriched.

The notion that there is more than one way of expanding one's knowledge about something is related to the work of Charles E. Lindblom and David Cohen (1979) on professional social inquiry. They distinguish between analytical and interactive problem solving, the latter referring to behavior to stimulate action so that an outcome occurs without requiring an analytical understanding or an analyzed solution. According to their argument, the alternatives employed in interactive problem solving are largely interactions among people, while analytical modes are to a great extent based on thought processes of individuals. As with our thesis, the modes are seen as complementary and not necessarily mutually exclusive endeavors. Also relevant here is Lotte Bailyn's (1977) concept of research as a cognitive process, contrasted to research as a validating process.

Additional support for this view is found in the research into the awareness process of chess masters by the Dutch psychologist A. Van deGroot (deGroot, 1965; Newell & Simon, 1972). He discovered that the masters think ahead in a detailed, analytical way but differ from novices in their ability to recall recognizable stimulus patterns of greater complexity. These patterns, or "chunks," as Newell and Simon called them, seem to be the basis for intuitive judgments by the masters, judgments that involve continuations or relationships that they cannot articulate. Masters differ from novices in the number of possible moves they review, but this is not the main factor in their differential success. What distinguishes them most significantly is that the masters have trained themselves to return repeatedly to the base position from which they started their analysis and, rather than to force a move, to allow the next move to "pop out" at them. A. Van deGroot referred to this as the process of progressive deepening.

Finally, the perspective advocated here is related to the Lewinian action research model in that both approaches regard data gathering as part of an ongoing, cyclical process rather than as something to be done so that the "real" work can commence.

Both suggest slow, tentative, successive refinement in the formulation of hypotheses. The major difference is that this approach places more emphasis on open, undirected awareness than do most action research practitioners, who seem to prefer the process of *active, directed awareness.* *

RETHINKING ASSUMPTIONS ABOUT THE GOALS OF DIAGNOSIS

In order to expand the perspective for organizational assessment beyond overreliance on active, directed awareness, several assumptions need to be examined:

1. That the goal of diagnosis is to identify specific causal factors that, once identified, determine the course of treatment. In complex systems that may be many factors that relate to define the functioning of the system. Thus, this assumption may not be realistic in such a setting. Much current thinking about illness and health, such as the various approaches to holistic medicine, suggests that this assumption is being questioned with regard to individual systems as well. A more useful assumption may be that the goal of diagnosis is to study the system, as much as is possible, until the interrelated factors are revealed. This process might be better called *assessment* than diagnosis.

2. That diagnosis is a separate step prior to intervention. This thinking leads to an artificial breakdown of a very complex process that moves along while diagnosis is taking place. One can easily relate to the notion that, as an intervention takes place, new data are created that were not available during the preintervention diagnostic phase. Consultants are always "surprised" by these occurrences, all of which imply that a preliminary diagnosis needs to be modified. Indeed, the method of action research requires a continuous process of planning an intervention following modified diagnosis based on the most current data available. This is nothing new to experienced clinicians, many of whom have stopped using clas-

*The interested reader is referred to Lewin (1946), Shepard (1960), and Whyte and Hamilton (1964) for discussions of the action research model.

sical nosologies for disease identification because such labeling blocks them from fully seeing and tracking the dynamics of their clients. Anna Freud once remarked that her diagnosis of a case was only completed at the point at which therapy was terminated. From this point of view, one may well argue that diagnosis can follow intervention, as well as the other way around.

3. That one's personal sensations, feelings, and internal states are less useful, and possibly harmful, to the diagnosis process, than are external observations and mental processing of such data. Self-awareness is one of the ways to gauge one's external world or to use as a basis for action. If I wish to engage my client, as opposed to defining and understanding the system, one of the most useful sources of information available in selecting an action is to give significant weight to what is happening inside me as I make contact with the system. Rationality and impersonality can be integrated with subjectivity and involvement.

4. That the job of the consultant is to diagnose the problem and recommend (and possibly implement) the appropriate solution. This is quite different from the assumption that the job of the consultant is to educate the client to do a better job of doing the work of diagnosis, solution determination, and implementation. If this is true, the aim of assessment, and of intervention, becomes one of teaching people how to give up data. The open, undirected approach assumes that the consultant does not initially know what data are critical, and does not care what data the system provides as long as the process of interacting with the system extracts the data needed to unblock the system and mobilize its energy to define and solve its own problems.

In developing the Columbo model in contrast to the Holmes model, I do not propose that the medical/scientific paradigm of 19th-century rationalism is a bad one, nor that it should be dropped. It would be silly to attempt entry into a complex work system without looking at the kinds of processes and structures that experience tells us are integral aspects of sound functioning. However, I do propose that the one-sided use of active, directed awareness supports a consultant role that is more like that of the disengaged scientist than the "producer-of-change-through-engagement." The value of the medical model has been great, to the point where it has unwittingly limited the vision of practitioners of organizational diagnosis and intervention. It is limiting to service-oriented, action research consultants in several ways:

1. The approach involves an overemphasis on what happened in the past and on cause–effect relationships, versus what is happening here-and-now (deterministic orientation versus existential orientation).
2. It overemphasizes a rational, analytic mode that restricts the awareness of the observer by directing the process to limited or biased channels (a point to be elaborated on later).
3. There is an overemphasis on intellectual understanding of the problem before allowing movement into action, restricting the interventionist to a partially disengaged position vis-à-vis the client, and reinforcing more consultant marginality than is useful.
4. Up to now, this approach has supported data gathering by surveys and interviews, and has minimized use of participant observation and unobtrusive measures such as are employed by the ethnographically oriented.
5. Despite statements by proponents of this model that they are looking for strengths as well as weaknesses in the systems they are studying, the model tends to focus unduly on the illness rather than on the health of the system.

INTEGRATING THE TWO MODELS

The Gestalt approach to awareness acknowledges use of both *active, directed awareness* (Holmes) and *open, undirected awareness* (Columbo). The Gestalt-oriented consultant is trained to use both modes. Neither awareness-enhancing approach is to be preferred over the other; good practice dictates moving back and forth between focus and sponge, keeping one's boundaries as open as possible to receive any and all data from self and other. Doing so seems best supported if one assumes that the goal of assessment is not to define the problem in order to make a solving intervention, but to find those issues that pique consultant interest and energy, and to see which mobilize the interest and energy of the client system. Intervention then becomes a process of "working" these awarenesses on both sides.

Some examples of open, undirected awareness in organizational assessment may help to convey its usefulness:

Case One

About three years ago I was asked to work with a subsidiary of one of my clients. This regional organization operates seven large depots, or stores, and a central purchasing and warehouse operation, serving the oil field exploration and drilling industry. After negotiating an assessment phase, I began touring the locations, armed only with some preliminary knowledge of the organization and its business, and some general areas to look at in assessing current functioning. After completing an interview at the third location, I walked out on the loading dock and waited for the store manager, who was late for his interview. A vice president who happened to be at the site in another connection offered to find the store manager for me since I had never met him and did not know what he looked like. As it was a sunny, spring day I walked around the supply yard and absorbed the activities taking place. I noticed a huge flatbed truck being loaded with pipe by two men, who then got into the truck and started driving away. The vice president came running out into the yard, waving his arms and shouting for the truck to stop; the store manager was one of the two men ready to drive out to make a delivery to an oil rig. No amount of interview questioning could have possibly conveyed the meaning of this scene. My internal reactions to the lack of discipline that marked this event added immeasurably to the data as to how at least one store manager's job is defined.

Case Two

In conducting an interview that lasted almost five hours and included dinner, I realized that my informant had not answered about a dozen questions, having deflected the point of the inquiry. After two hours I became painfully aware of how tired and heavy I was feeling. The informant had been highly touted to me by top management as being one of its best younger managers, and one who could help me a great deal with his views of the organization and its functioning. After dinner I finally said that I had been working very hard to obtain answers to what seemed very straightforward questions. This statement was responded to with another inconsequential, noncontactful deflection. Since I am very skilled at making good contact with relative strangers in difficult situations, I filed away for later use the experience of failing to make more than cursory contact with a person presumed to be very important to the organizational change effort upon which I was embarking. I had several pages of notes concerning aspects of the organization's functioning, none of which interested me as much as the noncontactful nature of this long exchange.

Case Three

In the course of teaching organizational assessment, I generally ask students to do an exercise in which they must spend some time in a place with no particular data-gathering requirement other than to keep all their senses open and not to ask any questions or otherwise converse with anyone. The task is simply to let things into their experience, whatever they might be. (After sharing their experiences, I ask the students to make up a list of questions they should like to pursue if they were to continue further assessment in that setting.) Here are some typical responses to this exercise.

- After walking around the cultural center of a large Midwestern city: "The most compelling thing was how few people were walking around" . . . "I felt that I was surrounded by a discrete, isolated bastion" . . . "the buildings are attractive but different from one another, like they just got added on somehow."
- After walking around a building housing a very successful educational institution: "The furniture is obviously inexpensive" . . . "the private offices are all different in style and arrangement" . . . . "I got a sense of fading elegance, perhaps of genteel poverty."
- After sitting for a while in an office area housing a department of a university: "I've been in that office many times during the past two years for some purpose or another, but I never noticed what is on the walls; they are mostly filled with old newspaper clippings."

The Gestalt-oriented assessor of systems sees the functions of assessment as follows:

1. To develop figural elements; to look for something(s) in which you and the client have interest: What do I "care about?" What does the client "care about?"

2. To become gounded personally; to reduce one's own inevitable confusion, uncertainty, anxiety, etc., when entering any new system.

3. To begin to teach the system how to give you data; to set a nonjudgmental model for rewarding any data people are willing to articulate and make public.

4. To estimate the client's present level of awareness of its process for dealing with the problem(s) at hand.

5. Selectively, to share data as a means of establishing good contact with the client system; to make your presence felt.

6. To test the potential for a useful working relationship by attempting to complete a small piece of work as part of the assessment.

This model embraces focused diagnostic techniques and adds some important components. Engagement with the system of study is both more open and more contactful, and it places a heavy weight upon the consultant's sensations, emotions, and other awareness. It requires a well-developed ability to attend to and observe oneself, as well as the client system. In addition, it requires the willingness and ability to be personally "up front" with one's observations, to treat data as a basis of hypothesis formation, rather than for confident conclusions, and to view assessment as taking place continuously as consultant and system interact. This consultant style is highly involving and oriented toward mobilization of energy in the client (remember that Columbo always stimulates, arouses, or motivates his potential adversary in some way.) It is an integrative model in which consultant and client work together to change something. It goes one step beyond a classical process consultation model in that the use of the full self and active presence of the consultant is a key component.

Figure 6-1 presents the Gestalt orientation toward organizational assessment. It is a perspective for the service-oriented, action-research practitioner that embodies the modes of the medically oriented diagnostician, the process consultant, and the ethnographer's participant-observation. It adds to the frame-

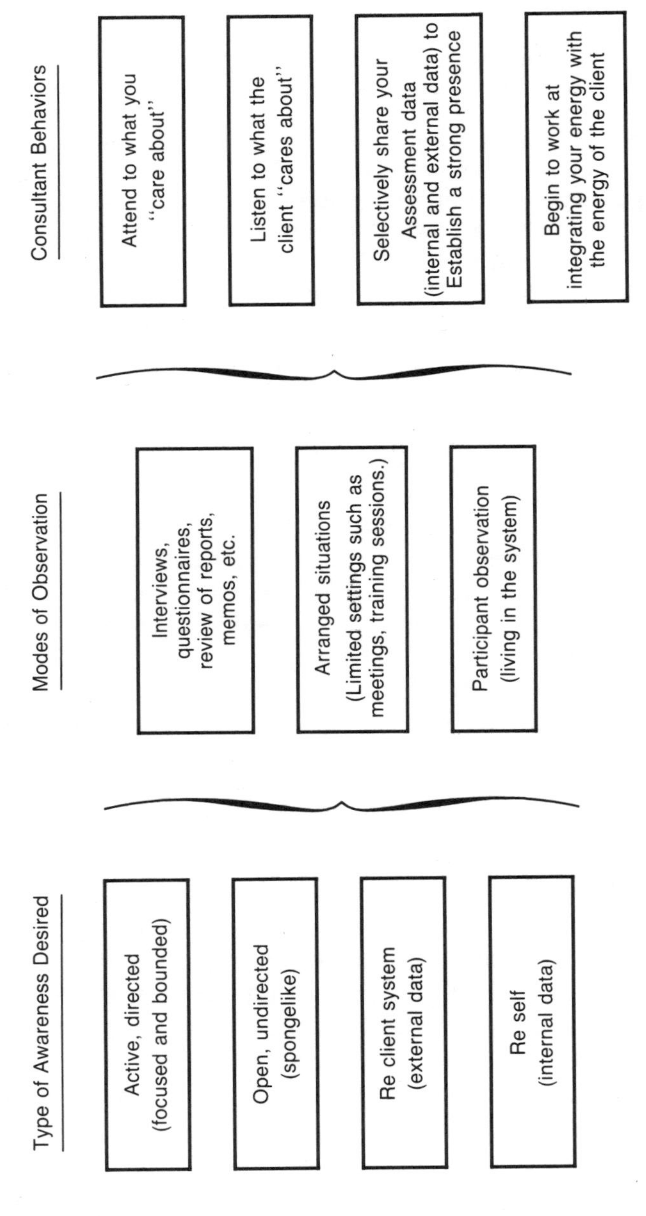

Figure 6-1. Gestalt perspective for organizational assessment.

work of these approaches a significant emphasis upon open awareness and uses self-awareness, as well as awareness of the other, as a measuring instrument, In this way the domain of assessment is enlarged.

IMPLICATIONS

The perspective presented here suggests an important shift in the practice of organizational consulting. To begin with, the objectives of the entry and contracting stages change. Working from the Holmesian approach, the consultant negotiates for an opportunity to make a study of the situation and to report back findings and recommendations for action steps. From the perspective of the Columbo model, the negotiation is for an opportunity to interact with the client system, as though to say: "Let's see what happens when we live together for a while." This does not rule out data gathering of a focused nature but it does significantly slow down movement to establish the consultant as an impersonal provider of analysis and the client as an object of study. It gives the system more opportunity to be seen, heard, and appreciated for what it is and, by feeding back small observations of system and of self as the interaction develops, there is greater opportunity to enlarge the client's energy for the undertaking. There is less need to feel dependent on some later pronouncement of the consultant before anything can happen. The result is a highly contactful interaction between consultant and client early in a relationship. The consultant is more concerned with testing for awareness and energy potentials in the system than in making a correct diagnosis of a problem.

Achieving the kind of relationship proposed by this approach will not be easy; the client may be hurting badly and may believe that the consultant is an expert who can quickly come up with the right "medicine." However, we need to realize that every time we agree to a contract emphasizing short, quick data collection followed by an intervention based on this data, we are reinforcing the medical model and minimizing our opportunities to collect the kind of data that can only emerge through less focused interaction or participant-observation.

The consultant who wishes to improve skills in assessment and high-impact intervention needs to become well grounded in the method of open awareness as well as in conceptual frameworks of how organizations function. Tichy and Nisberg (1976) have written at length on how bias leads to a change agent asking certain questions and not others, resulting in an imbalanced picture of an organization. This bias stems from relatively tightly bound choices by the interventionist as to the change model preferred and is a reflection of the values, needs, and orientation of the consultant. We do have a strong tendency in the Western world to choose quickly what to attend to, and to make premature organization of the field of study. I know of no other way to compensate for these biasing tendencies than to train ourselves to be as open, nonjudgmental, and receptive as we can become to what is out there in the world of the system with which we are engaging. This is a difficult learning endeavor for the highly experienced practitioner—it is very hard not to "know" what you want to look at when you have seen many, many situations over time—but this is what Gestalt methodology attempts to make possible by enlarging the scope of organizational assessment.

REFERENCES

Bailyn, L. "Research as a cognitive process: Implications for data analysis." *Quality and Quantity*, 11 (1977), 97–117.

Baring-Gould, W.S. *The Annotated Sherlock Holmes*. New York: Crown, 1967.

Beckhard, R. "The dynamics of the consulting process in large system change." Sloan School Working Paper 730-74, August 1974.

Beckhard, R., and Harris, R. *Organizational Transitions: Managing Complex Change*. Reading, Mass.: Addison-Wesley, 1977.

deGroot, A.D. *Thought and Choice in Chess*. The Hague: Mouton, 1965.

Levinson, H. *Organizational Diagnosis*. Cambridge, Mass.: Harvard University Press, 1972.

Lewin, K. "Action research and minority problems." *Journal of Social Issues*, 2, no. 4 (1946), 34–36.

Likert, R. *New Patterns of Management.* New York: McGraw-Hill, 1961.

Lindblom, C.E., and Cohen, D.K. *Usable Knowledge.* New Haven: Yale University Press, 1979.

Mahler, W.R. *Diagnostic Studies.* Reading, Mass.: Addison-Wesley, 1974.

Nadler, D.A. *Feedback and Organization Development: Using Data-Based Methods.* Reading, Mass.: Addison-Wesley, 1974.

Newell, A., and Simon, H.A. *Human Problem-Solving.* Englewood Cliffs, N.J.: Prentice-Hall, 1972.

Ornstein, R., *The Psychology of Consciousness.* New York: Harcourt Brace, Jovanovich, 1977.

Perls, F., Hefferline, R.F., and Goodman, R. *Gestalt Therapy.* New York: Julian Press, 1951.

Polster, E., and Polster, M. *Gestalt Therapy Integrated.* New York: Bruner/Mazel, 1973.

Schein, E. "The role of the consultant: Content expert or process facilitator?" Sloan School of Management Paper, June 1977.

Schein, E. *Process Consultation.* Reading, Mass.: Addison-Wesley, 1969.

Shepard, H.A. "An action research model," in *An Action Research Program for Organization Improvement.* Ann Arbor, Mich.: Foundation for Research on Human Behavior, University of Michigan, 1960.

Tichy, N.M., and Nisberg, J.N. "Change agent bias: What they view determines what they do." *Group & Organization Studies,* September 1976 (3), 286–301.

Truzzi, M. "Sherlock Holmes as Applied Social Psychologist." In Sanders, *The Sociologist as Detective.* New York: Praeger, 1976, pp. 50–86.

Weisbord, M.R. "Organization diagnosis: Six places to look for trouble with or without a theory." *Group & Organization Studies,* December 1976 (4), 430–447.

Weisbord, M.R. *Organizational Diagnosis.* Reading, Mass.: Addison-Wesley, 1978.

Whyte, W.F., and Hamilton, E.L. *Action Research for Management.* Homewood, Ill.: Irwin Dorsey, 1964.

Zinker, J. *Creative Process in Gestalt Therapy.* New York: Vintage Books, 1978.

7 Evocative and Provocative Modes of Influence in the Implementation of Change*

THE MEANING OF INFLUENCE

This chapter expands on the discussions of presence, desired skills, and Gestalt awareness process. The focus is on how the consultant acts on his or her awareness, and how skill and presence combine to encourage or produce client action. The choices or alternatives available to consultants for stimulating or influencing client action are specifically considered. Before examining these alternatives, it will help to look at the meaning of influence in the consulting relationship.

Anyone who has ever tried to influence others while carrying out a professional role has struggled with questions such as the following.

- How do I act in order to be influential?
- What strategies or tactics for being influential seem com-

* This chapter is an expanded version of an article that appeared in *The Gestalt Journal*, vol. VI, no. 2, Fall 1983. Permission to draw upon this material has been granted by *The Gestalt Journal*.

fortable to me? (What are my guiding assumptions concerning the exercise of influence over others?)

- How "mild" or "strong" an effort is required in a given situation?
- What response will satisfy me as being worth my efforts?
- How shall I deal with my frustration or confusion if my efforts to influence do not seem to be working well?
- How will I know that I have been truly influential? (What are my needs/criteria for confirmation or validation as an instrument of influence?)

These questions, and others like them, make up the core of what it means to be influential. In particular, they call for sharp focus on the use of self as an instrument of influence, and on how the personal experience of the consultant is a potent factor in this endeavor. Awareness of one's own immediate experience, and the ability to use this in here-and-now interaction with the client system, become the key skills for the practitioner of influence. The use of self is defined as the way in which one acts upon one's observations, values, feelings, and so forth, in order to have an effect on the other. This includes the articulation of awareness of all kinds, such as feelings and sensations, thoughts, images, and fantasies.

How a consultant observes and acts in an influential way—indeed, what is observed and attended to—depends to a large extent on how the goals of intervention are defined. On the one hand, the consultant may decide to focus on a clear *outcome* or end-state for the target system, and thus may develop an "investment" in the attainment of that specific goal. On the other hand, the goal for the consultant may be the achievement of system *interest* in something he or she considers important, but which the system does not yet view as an interesting issue or an interesting way of looking at a problem or process. In the second instance, specific outcomes are less critical to the consultant than is the enhancement of the system's awareness of choices or alternatives that derive from heightened consciousness. These are not mutually exclusive goals, but they do refer to different points of the Gestalt Cycle of Experience. The concern for achievement of an outcome directs consultant attention and energy to the *action and contact* stages; the concern for generating interest directs attention and energy to the *awareness* stage of the Cycle. If intervenors characteristically value one objective over the other, they are likely to have preferences for varying modes of exerting influence, and preference for different ways in which to use themselves for this purpose. This becomes an important determinant of strategies for influencing others and it shapes the consultant's stance.

TWO MODES OF INFLUENCE

Studies of change agents of all kinds reveal two major modes that predominate in the strategic stances that follow from preference for one intervention goal or the other: the *provocative mode* and the *evocative mode*. The provocative mode draws on a belief that system outcomes are what count if one is to be influential in actuality, and that nothing of real consequence can occur unless the intervenor causes, or forces, something to happen. In this mode compelling intervenor behavior drives toward specific actions by the system and rests upon a strong desire to achieve a reaction within a fairly narrow band of possible actions, one that is tightly bounded in the eyes of the intervenor. Strong actions are taken that are designed to jolt, or intrude upon, the system's awareness so that the system moves rapidly to produce action in response.

In the evocative mode, the consultant strives to get the system interested in what it is doing, what is being attended to by the members of the system, and what the process being used is. To evoke means to bring about a shift in what is attended to by the system; the goal is the creation of fresh awareness and the education of the system to be more effective in its awareness processes. There is greater willingness on the part of the intervenor to allow the client system to remain at the awareness stage of the Cycle of Experience and to let client actions *emerge*. The aim is for the intervenor to be arousing but not unsettling.

William S. Warner referred to this mode as "therapist as evocateur."*

We see, then, that to be influential requires that a consultant use himself or herself in an important way, but that there are divergent methods of doing so. The provocative may be seen as a *forcing* approach; the evocative mode is best described as an *emergent* approach. Table 7-1 lists the qualities that distinguish the two modes. In reviewing these distinctions, it is important to recognize that both can be applied usefully with the same client, they are merely different tactical means of actualizing a strategic choice as to how the client system can best be helped to energize itself.

Before looking at how the modes apply to the consulting setting, it will further understanding to discuss them in terms of broader social change. While it is more customary to think of provocative means, such as actions in support of revolutionary changes, careful analysis reveals a range of behaviors and consequences make up this mode. One can be provocative without being assaultative or a terrorist; confrontation need not be violent—as was demonstrated in the community organizing techniques of Saul Alinsky (1972). One of his favorite actions was to have a large group of people enter into the space of a store or a corporation considered to be slack in affirmative action programs. This action almost always obtained a reaction from the target group and it is qualitatively a very different provocation than a kidnapping or a bombing. While it may result in anger on the part of the recipient, it does not necessarily lead to violent or strongly aggressive retaliation. Thus in the provocative mode, the agent of change can put himself or herself "on the line" with varying degrees of risk and consequence. The ultimate use of self, of course, can be to risk life itself. I use the labels *confrontation* and *assault* to capture the difference be-

* Warner, as part of the first group at the Gestalt Institute of Cleveland to be influenced and trained by Fritz Perls, Laura Perls, and Isadore From, quickly grasped this distinction, being inherently a polished evocateur. The evocative mode was further refined and developed by the members of the Cleveland group—who were able to separate out the power of the mode from the provocative aspects of Fritz Perls' early work—and made a cornerstone of what became known as the "Cleveland style," in contrast to the more provocative aspects of what some have called the "California style," or "therapist as provocateur."

Table 7-1. Behavioral Qualities of Evocative and Provocative Modes of Using Self as an Instrument of Influence

Evocative Mode	*Provocative Mode*
Behavior that shows or enhances your way of being in the world	Actions that make something happen; cause something to occur.
Behavior of the consultant that brings forth something from the client, but the response is client-directed and often not predictable by the consultant	An active, directed intervention; planned or sharply focused behavior designed to force client to attend to something specific
Behavior creating conditions—such as trust, hope, safety, vision—that allow excitement or interest to grow in others	Actions that break up or violate understanding, expectations, or contracts between or among people
Display of your skills or values without disrupting the functioning of the client system	Actions that interrupt the normal functioning of the system's procedures or structures
Actions that "break up" the client's awareness but still leave room for the client to choose its own actions	Actions that force or require the client to change its actions
Actions that do not compel a particular response, or to which the client system need not make a direct response	The client can hardly avoid responding; must do something in reaction to the behavior

tween the Alinsky-type approach and more violent acts such as coercion or terrorism.

Just as there are two variations in provocative behavior, we may distinguish two degrees or types of evocative behavior. Perhaps the most passive and seemingly mildest form is pure *modeling*. Here one simply is who or what one is and has only a general hope that "doing my own thing" becomes of interest to the client. In this form influence rests upon the subtlest of forces but, as we know from the literature on modeling and social learning theory, can be quite powerful. The research on child development and the work of Albert Bandura (1963, 1976) on behavior modeling have more than demonstrated this power. Closely allied to modeling, but involving a less passive, more focused form of evocation, is *elicitation*—consultant behavior designed to encourage or bring out a more specific response.

These actions are less forcing than confrontation and allow the client to choose not to respond in action and to remain at the awareness level. The techniques of client-centered therapy that direct the client inward and away from externals (such as reflecting back client comments, insistence upon saying "you") are examples of this variation. The use of metaphor and other poetic modes falls within this category. Likewise, the cognitive inputs of many speeches and much formal teaching are examples of more directed consciousness raising through evocation. While it is true that the use of these behaviors is an aspect of modeling, the focus is more directed, and the energy employed by the user to reach the client is stronger than in pure modeling.

The ease with which provocative examples can be found in social change efforts does not mean that evocative modes are lacking at this level. On the contrary, numerous significant social changes have come about through the power of attractive life-styles or compelling nonprovocative presences. The teachings and life-style of Buddha, the fasting and otherwise ascetic life of Ghandi, the wartime speeches of Winston Churchill, and Martin Luther King's "I Have a Dream" speech are all examples of the evocative mode on a grand scale. In this regard it is interesting that Daniel Ellsberg's response to being called a hero by multitudes of college students for his release of the Vietnam war-related "Pentagon Papers" (a highly provocative act) was to say: "Better that all of you simply stand clearly and strongly for what you are and what you believe in than to rely on single acts of great provocation by someone who happens to be in a unique position to take this kind of risk" (Ellsberg, 1974).

Analysis of the typical range of consultant–client interactions indicates few examples of *assaultative* provocation, though coercive efforts to make system members comply with a change often make the consultant an accomplice to what may be seen as a highly provocative act. There are certain kinds of therapy, such as the Synanon approach to drug addiction and the est programs that rely on strongly unsettling or attacking methods to evoke a client response. Given the nature of the employment contract of most internal and external consultants, it is unusual to find client organizations "brutalized" to any degree; indeed, professional codes of ethics make strong statements about the unacceptability of such behavior.

On the other hand, what I have labeled *confrontative* provocation is to be found frequently where effective consultation is practiced. When a consultant chooses to challenge the client through the sharing of feelings and emotions of any kind, through the use of disagreement, through statements of interpretation or fantasies that stretch or push at the client's boundaries, or through persistent demands for certain client behavior, this mode is being applied. The confrontation meeting, the actions of a third-party intervenor, and assertiveness training programs are applications of confrontative provocation. The key element is that the recipient of the action feels some pressure to respond to such a direct intervention, but is not prevented from carrying on with normal functioning. These approaches act both to enlarge the client's awareness and to push the system toward action, but they enable a more reasoned, controlled action to take place than in the case of *assaultative* provocation. The system can just take in the experience and not do anything at that point; it can decide whether to maintain or change its boundaries in response, even though it may experience pressure to move.

One way to understand the evocative mode in consulting is to consider organizational assessment or diagnosis as resting largely upon its use. The aim is to enhance the awareness of both consultant and client within the context of a basic faith that this activity will lead to emergent aciton. The asking of questions in organizational assessment serves to focus the client's attention on what the system is doing, and shares with the client what is interesting to the consultant (as manifested in the areas and questions put to the system). Likewise, survey feedback interventions are designed to be evocative.

Table 7-2 summarizes the examples of these modes in both social change efforts and consulting situations. The four variations are grouped as though there is a continuum running from *modeling* at one end, through *elicitation* and *confrontative provocation*, to *assaultative provocation* at the other end. The evocative end point represents larger intervenor investment in *awareness* goals, and the assaultative end reflects stronger intervenor investment in *action or outcome* goals, with much less

Table 7-2. Examples of Provocative and Evocative Modes of the Use of Self in Change Efforts

Evocative Mode		*Provocative Mode*	
Modeling	*Elicitation*	*Confrontation*	*Assault*
Buddha's life style	Confucius' *Analects*	Evangelical preaching	Coercive persuasion
Ghandi's ascetic life	Tao Te Ching	Boycotts and sit-ins (e.g., Ghandi, King's bus boycott)	Draft card burning
Utopian communities; social experiments that may be observed by others; trend-setting, new lifestyles	Client-centered counseling	Techniques of S. Alinsky	Terrorist acts such as bombing, kidnapping, airplane hijacking
Apprenticeship learning arrangements	Teaching through the lecture method	Peaceful demonstrations	Wildcat strikes, Clamshell Alliance break-ins at Seabrook Nuclear Facility
President Carter wearing a sweater, walking to the White House on Inauguration Day	M. L. King's speeches	Strong rhetoric; propaganda	D. Ellsberg's release of the Pentagon papers to the press
President Reagan wearing Western-style clothes and riding a horse	Use of rich language: metaphor, imagery, poetic modes, gestures	M. L. King's protest marches	Synanon therapy
Being attractive in manner/style, so as to draw attention, interest	President Reagan saying "there is no energy shortage in this great land of ours" (paraphrase of his remarks)	Sadat's historic trip to Jerusalem (1977)	Rolfing
Vicarious learning, observing without trying or simply by being in the same space with another	Asking questions or making remarks that gain the attention of others	Encounter groups	est programs
	Awareness-enhancing techniques, such as those used in Gestalt therapy, psychosynthesis, synectics, body therapies (Alexander, Feldenkrais, etc.)	Assertiveness training	Acts that browbeat or "rape" others into responding; any act of hostility or an act that strongly violates an agreement
		Tavistock Group	
		Confrontation meetings	
		Bioenergetics	
		Third-party intervention	
		Interpreting another's behavior to them	
		Statements to clients that stretch, or go beyond, established boundaries	

concern for the development of emergent actions by the system. Elicitation and confrontation fall between these extremes.

At the extreme end of the evocative mode is what we might call pure modeling. In this variation influence is gained simply by the consultant and the client system occupying the same life space. The client may or may not be aware that modeling is taking place. The client undergoes vicarious learning by simply observing or watching the consultant as an adjunct to their job task fulfillment. This process goes on whether or not the consultant consciously attempts to gain influence through his or her way of being. What is observed or modeled ranges from specific skills, attitudes, and the use of language to more general things, such as overall manner, life-style, or the nature of the consultant's presence as a whole. Modeling is a form of the evocative mode in that the consultant's way of being evokes a response in the members of the client system. This response may vary among the client members, and it may be quite different from what the consultant expects. In any event, something is evoked simply by the consultant being present. It is literally impossible for the consultant not to be an evocateur; he or she can evoke negative or positive reactions in others but cannot be ignored. This is why presence is so powerful as a means of being influential.

The examples in Table 7-2 for the provocative modes make greater reference to strong directed actions. The evocative process is subtler and relies much less on specific linkages than does the provocative. What the client responds to is not necessarily predictable, and the response itself may be one of many possibilities. For example, though the consultant may have a friendly, convivial manner, it might evoke suspicion or mistrust in the client system, as opposed to trust and openness. A noncommital, taciturn consultant might evoke anger in the client system or curiosity as to what the consultant is thinking but not saying. Furthermore, these aspects of consultant behavior may have little or no significant evocative power with a given client, and some other aspect—perhaps the consultant's reputation—may have a stronger impact in arousing client openness. In any case a response is obtained even if the stimuli that help to elicit it are not obvious. The cues are subtle and often not in the awareness of either the consultant or the members of the client system. Moreover, forces in the client have much to do with what is evoked and a particular response may say as much about the client as it does about the consultant.

ILLUSTRATIONS OF BOTH MODES IN THE CONSULTING PROCESS

Several of the case examples presented earlier in this book help to illustrate the two modes. The case of Jack, the president of a family business (Chapter 3), is a good example of confrontative provocation following a period of modeling and elicitation. The case of team building with the nutritionists (Chapter 3) is an example of an attempt at modeling that went awry. All three cases concerning presence in Chapter 4 are examples of the evocative mode. The following cases will further clarify and contrast the modes.

Case One

A number of years ago, I consulted with a group of three men who had formed a partnership to invest in and acquire businesses. Prior to this, I had spent about a year working primarily with one of the men and his subordinate executives on management and organization issues in their growing holdings. To gain a better idea of their goals and mode of operation, I was invited to sit in and observe their biweekly partners' meeting and the board meetings of one of their companies. For several months I said very little at these meetings, which were long, poorly organized, and constantly interrupted by telephone calls. After a while, I became quite tense and restless, but still I offered only a few pleasantries or asked a few questions to clarify something they were discussing. Occasionally I was asked to report briefly on my work within their organizations. The partners seemed quite content to have me observe them in action; they never asked me for any feedback on the process or structure of their meeting.

The 12th meeting was particularly bad—actions were being considered that involved millions of dollars but for which

> there had been little preparation, the interruptions were constant, and it was still very disorganized. As one of the participants returned after having left to take a telephone call, I could no longer contain myself and I stopped the discussion to say in no uncertain terms that I thought their meetings were among the worst I had ever seen, that I would never be as nonchalant about making decisions involving my money as they were, and that I could not see how they could make good decisions while operating in this fashion. After a moment of what was, for me, an agonizing silence, they responded by asking what I meant. In retrospect, I can only guess that the reason they did not react to my outburst by throwing me out of the room was that they had begun to respect and trust me. At any rate, I had stopped the action of their meeting through use of *confrontative provocation*. I used this break to ask how they felt about their process, and they stated that they were not entirely happy with it but just accepted it as an inherent cost. As would be expected, it turned out that each thought he was the only one who found the process difficult and sometimes annoying. I asked them if they wanted help from me in developing a better process, and they agreed to try out a few changes in future sessions. They subsequently improved their meetings considerably, although they never completely changed the basic pattern until one partner left the group several years later.

In analyzing this example, it is important to realize that my intervention was not a planned, calculated move. It grew out of my tension and a need to do something to shake up the existing pattern. Until just a few minutes prior to my statement, I had no idea that I might intervene to stop the meeting. For months I simply presented myself as an interested, quiet participant. At best I was seen as some kind of model to observe. It is hard to believe that this type of intervention will work without the support that comes from building a relationship over time. While there are instances where aggressive, confrontational moves help to build the relationship, generally some basis of trust must exist so that the client system will give consent to or accept a more jarring move by a consultant. Finally, the intervention should be seen as one in which awareness of the client system is heightened, but in a way that influences action by the client system. The impact on action takes this response out of the evocative mode. They could have ignored me and continued with the meeting, but I made this difficult for them to do. That it was not impossible for them to go on allows us to label this an instance of *confrontative provocation*, rather than assaultative. The latter requires a more coercive move to which a response cannot be avoided.

Case Two

> For the past two years, I have been doing some general consulting with a medium-sized manufacturing company, having known the chief executive officer through a previous assignment at another firm. The work involves, among other things, being part of a top management committee on executive selection and development, and the design and conduct of executive retreats. During this period many changes have taken place in this organization as part of a turnaround situation. At a recent meeting of the executive development committee in which some business setbacks were discussed, I noticed that the CEO seemed tired and somewhat depressed; he is normally optimistic and upbeat in his manner. When the meeting ended and we were saying goodbye, I mentioned that it appeared he had a lot on his mind, and I asked if there was any way I could help. He responded half-seriously by asking if I was concerned about his mental health. I immediately replied that I would call him later to set up a date to see him alone. Two days later we met for breakfast, and he unburdened himself about the serious nature of two or three of his business problems and how these were beginning to get him down after almost three years of herculean, generally successful, efforts to revitalize his company. I mainly listened or made supportive remarks that acknowledged his feelings and the fact that they had a strong basis in reality. At the end of the meeting, I said that it seemed that his problems were going to be with him for quite a while, and that he might be running himself down by working long, hard stretches without breaks. I teased him into agreeing to spend more time with family and social contacts and to take some long weekends. I had no illusion that these simple "bromides" would solve his problems in any way other than to help by focusing his awareness on whether he was supporting himself well during a difficult time. I did not expect more than a modest response to my suggestion, but I thought that it was a start. In this regard it is important to know that this executive has a highly alert, inquisitive mind, and that he listens to

and remembers almost everything said to him by his associates.

This example falls both in the *elicitation* and *confrontative* modes. It was elicitation when I asked the CEO if he wanted anything from me, and when I reflected back and supported his feelings of discouragement during our breakfast meeting. Suggesting that he attend to his support systems was another example. The confrontation was mainly in my saying that we should get together, and in my calling him to set up the breakfast meeting, rather than waiting for him to call me. The initial confrontation was when I first told him that he appeared tired and depressed (basically an interpretation on my part). I used confrontation to get his attention quickly, and fell back to elicitation once we had established better contact.

Case Three

One of the most difficult decisions for a consultant comes up when a client system is about to act in a way that the consultant believes is deleterious to the system. Where system learning is an important goal of the client–consultant relationship, one can make a convincing argument for allowing the action to proceed without intervention if the cost is not obviously devastating. On the other hand, one can argue that there are many lessons that can be learned, and that the price of any failure in a system which is struggling to improve itself is too high to pay at any time. This case is an example of the use of confrontation based on consultant belief that a contemplated action would undo months of hard-gained trust and seriously undermine an organization development effort.

The case involves a possible decision to postpone a meeting set as a follow-up to a three-day management retreat. The retreat, which was the culmination of several months of preliminary work in developing organizational objectives and a fresh approach to management style, was very successful. However, immediately following the retreat, several events within the business of this organizaiton (a subsidiary of a larger firm) and at the corporate level put great pressure on the managers involved to put aside everything else and concentrate on the two problems identified.When I called the person in charge of arranging the one-day follow-up to get details con-

> cerning time and place, I was told that there were rumors of postponing the meeting. I was very upset by this news, largely because it would be an enormous setback to the organization development that was under way. The managers at the retreat were all engaged in follow-up action assignments that came out of the retreat; their enthusiasm and progress would be lost, perhaps irrevocably, if the meeting were canceled. In addition, I had gone to great effort to make myself available to this organization over the past year, and I experienced irritation with this turn of events. After wrestling with my irritation for a day or so, and telling myself that I was becoming too concerned with outcomes, I decided that I would intervene. I called the president and told him that unless he had some overpowering reason for canceling the meeting, he would be making a big mistake by calling it off. He said that he did not want to call it off but was concerned about taking 20 managers off the job for a full day at this point. We discussed this for a while, during which I did not budge from my point that the meeting should take place and we decided to schedule two, four-hour sessions over a ten-day period.

This example is important in that it calls into question the possible difference between doing process consultation and giving of advice. More precisely, the question is whether one does not offer advice until it is asked for, or gives it unsolicited in the hope that it will help the client. I do not claim that what I did in this case was a model response; my personal feelings and biases were all too apparent to me. But I decided that there was a risk that elicitation would not be useful in getting the meeting to take place, and that confrontation would be.

IMPLICATIONS

If the evocative mode has the kind of power suggested here, the influence of the consultant may depend as much on an ability to elicit or bring forth the broadest array of possible responses in others than on any single action or structure in the situation. Whether specific advice is heard or listened to, the extent to which client systems are willing to consider stretching boundaries or a new possibility may, in the final analysis, depend more on day-in, day-out intervenor presence and forces evoked than on identifiable acts of provocation. Daniel Ellsberg may be correct in his judgment to this effect; certainly, if one chooses to work for change within the system, there is much less likelihood of generating counterforce if evocative modes are used to their fullest potential. Yet it is not necessary to choose between the two *if confrontative provocation is employed rather than the assaultative mode.* The assaultative mode gives provocation a bad name, largely because of the violent, coercive actions involved. But even though nonviolent provocation may receive a violent response—as with the Selma protest march of Martin Luther King and his followers—confrontation between parties committed to a common goal may provide just enough spark to set off useful action. Here the risk being taken by the intervenor is based on reasonable probability of working out well, or it allows for a retreat if the action misses the mark or is more than the recipient can handle at that moment. In most assaultative acts, this is not the case and risks often take on an all-or-nothing quality.

It may well be that a feasible intervention sequence emphasizes the evocative mode first and works up to use of confrontative provocation with a more aware, interested, and "primed" client system. Particularly where a great deal of confusion or anxiety exists in a system, creation of an atmosphere that facilitates emergent action may work better than one that forces the action. If so, this suggests that in many organization change efforts the developmental/learning approach of evocative-derived action might precede the political-like tactics or action strategies of the provocative mode. This is close to the process in the first case above and to the cases described in Chapter 4. The problem with this in many situations is that it takes time to allow this sequence to flourish, and the approach may not manifest enough force to produce action quickly where action is seen as imperative, or where a jolt is useful to enlarge client awareness. On the other hand, while the provocative approach certainly speeds things up, it can be perceived as so forceful and attacking that it generates counterforce and resistance of another kind.

Both modes have significant values and limitations; artful consultation requires sensitive and intelligent balancing. In two of the above cases, confrontative provocation was used in single, specific moments, followed by elicitation and modeling. In these instances strong counterforce did not emerge—in one case because the confrontation was supportive in tone, and in both because trust in the consultant had been developed. Without one of these conditions, the provocative mode is more risky.

These considerations refer to phenomena that have been dealt with before by others. It is hoped that the framework presented here illuminates new insights as to how to be influential in a consulting role. Those who have hesitated to be highly confrontative may draw some support to be more provocative in this vein. Those who have been action oriented, putting their energies largely into programmatic concerns and end-states, may put more value on staying at the awareness level and learning to be influential without trying too hard. Change can occur, or influence may be felt by the client, by simply using the power of "being," and what one is. An interesting comment by Maimonides (1881), in *Guide for the Perplexed*, states that the only way to explain why some of the Commandments appeared is that they were put there to *evoke obedience* to God for its own sake, and not for any further specific reason. Extrapolated to consulting work, the message suggests that the process of evocation is at least as important as directing focus on the content of the issues people grapple with in their working lives. Failure to respect this wisdom and the power of the evocative mode results in overvaluing the content issues of the work and tends to support pushing for change. The growing interest by consultants in Eastern philosophy and the current research on modeling and the role of mentors demonstrate enhanced interest in the importance of the evocative mode and of not rushing the awareness pahse. However, as patience wanes and frustration increases in response to the difficulty of achieving change goals in a complex world, we see growing tendencies to resort to the "all-or-nothing," high-risk actions of assaultative provocation. The elicitation and confrontative modes show us that there are other ways to exert useful influence.

REFERENCES

Alinksy, S. *Rules for Radicals*, New York: Random House, 1972.

Bandura, A. "Social learning perspective on behavior change." In A. Burton, (ed.), *What Makes Behavior Change Possible?* New York: Brunner/Mazel, 1976, pp. 34–57.

Bandura, A., and Walter, R.H. *Social Change and Personality Development.* New York: Holt, Rinehart & Winston, 1963.

Ellsberg, D. Speech at the American Academy of Psychotherapists Conference, Cleveland, Ohio, 1974.

Lieberman, M.A., Yalom, I.P., and Miles, M.B. *Encounter Groups: First Facts*, New York: Basic Books, 1973.

Maimonides. *Guide for the Perplexed*, London: Trubner, 1881.

Warner, W.S. Unpublished lecture notes, Gestalt Institute of Cleveland, 1975.

8 On the Meaning of Resistance in Organizational Settings

Much has been written about the concept of resistance and how to deal with it. Since the time of Freud (1900), resistance has been a central issue for psychotherapy, and organization theorists have addressed the topic at great length for many years—including classic papers by Coch and French (1960) and Lawrence (1969). Despite this attention in early works and in more current interpretations, helping professionals show a great deal of confusion in the way they label, define, and work, with manifestations of resistance from or within client systems. There is probably no other issue that cries out for greater understanding by consultants. This chapter attempts to shed light on the meaning of resistance in organizational settings.

Resistance is a label applied by managers or consultants to the perceived behavior of others who seem unwilling to accept influence or help. It is a label provided by those who see themselves as agents of change, and is not necessarily the phenomenological experience of the targets. This simple, perhaps obvious, point is often overlooked, and most of the attempts to understand resistance are made from the perspective or bias of those seeking to bring about change. As Klein (1976) points out in his excellent article on change, Freud himself used the term to describe the blocking of attainment of his therapeutic objectives. Likewise, Lawrence (1954) offers advice on how to overcome resistance to change, but clearly accepts the orientation of the initiator of change as the starting point even though he is very sympathetic to the position of the targets. A more complete understanding of the phenomenon of resistance must include descriptions of the experience as felt and seen by the resisters as well as by the initiators of change. In a well-publicized article by Kotter and Schlesinger (1979), the four most common reasons why people resist change are listed.

1. A desire not to give up something of value.
2. A misunderstanding of the change and its implications.
3. A belief that the change does not make sense for the organization.
4. A low tolerance for change.

All but the last of these give credence to the fact that there may be legitimate differences in the way various members of the organization see the same situation. An even more useful perspective is provided by Klein (1976) in his conception of the role of the "defender," a term used to denote those spokespersons for the inner core of tradition and values who become forces against change—a mobilization he considers a prerequisite of successful change. Klein provides three reasons why defenders are useful in resisting change.

1. They are sensitive to any indication that those seeking to produce change fail to understand or identify with the core values of the system they seek to influence.
2. They see consequences of the change that are unanticipated by the initiators and that may threaten the well-being of the system.
3. They are especially apt to react to changes seen as reducing the integrity of the system; that is, they are sensitive to the importance of maintaining self-esteem, competence, and autonomy (Klein, 1976, p. 121).

From writings such as Klein's and others, we are drawn to the implication that "what usually passes for resistance is not just a dumb barrier to be removed but a creative force for managing a difficult world" (Polster & Polster, 1973). Even Freud pointed out that without resistance clients might become overwhelmed by the therapist's interventions. From the perspective of the initiator of change, resisters may be seen as being defensive, but from the perspective of the resisters, their behavior may very appropriately be seen as healthy self-regulation, or at least protective reaction to potential damage to their integrity.

A related, very critical point is that all resistance is mobilization of energy, not a lack of energy. In his work on force field analysis, Kurt Lewin (1951) makes it very clear that nonmovement of people toward a presumably desirable goal must be seen as a dynamic state, a quasistationary equilibrium composed of many opposing forces. Those who "resist" are to be seen as "bundles of energy," not as passive, lifeless blobs. I doubt if there is a single psychotherapist or consultant who has not marveled at the strength with which clients hold on to ways of being, or who has not despaired of being able to mount enough "counterforce" to help the client move to a new place. This phenomenon is also seen at the highest levels of organizational life, where top executives constantly complain that "my biggest problem is that I can't get anybody to do what I want." The people about whom this complaint is made are often high-level managers, including the most energetic, accomplishing members of the organization; it is just that their energies are pointed in different directions from that of the complainant. This is addressed in greater detail later.

Further confusion about resistance stems from the fact that those who experience it in the organizational setting see it through affective lenses; it is seen as expression of emotion and it generates emotional responses. This fails to recognize that all expressions of resistance may just as easily be viewed through cognitive lenses; what is happening is that information is being processed. In Gestalt parlance, work is going on at the awareness level of the Cycle of Experience, and data are being displayed showing that various individuals see different figural elements or are at different points on the Cycle with regard to mobilization of energy and action. If this is true, we recognize the beginnings of a view of the phenomenon of resistance as a potentially useful step in a decision-making process, perhaps leading to a better informed decision than is first presented. This, of course, is what Klein is getting at in his focus on the role of the defender.

From the above considerations, I come to a working hypothesis about resistance: *The expression of any indication of opposition to something is as much a statement of the integrity of the person(s) expressing it as is the manifestation of nonoppositional behavior.* Working from this premise shifts the field of interaction between the initiator and the resister from that of an incipient power struggle—with all the potential for intense conflict, passive aggression, sabotage, and so forth—to that of exploration of differences. If this premise is truly accepted by agents of change, it will be very difficult for them to see themselves as the "good guys" and the resisting targets as the "bad guys." Although this is readily grasped on an intellectual level by most helping professionals and by many managers, because so much often rides on outcome investment by the initiator of change, to engage in exploration of these differences is perceived as a loss of influence and as an invalidation of one's power or authority.

This leads to another critical point, namely, that resistance as a concept or as a manifestation has meaning only where there are power differentials among people. Those with less power cannot easily say "no" to something, and so they fall back on reactions that are then labeled as resistance. To understand this, we must recognize that to say "no" to something is not the same as to resist. To say "no" is a clear response that is made among presumed peers who have differences of interest or opinion. We can see this in union–management negotiations, an example of influence exchanges among relatively equal powers. While one side may look at the other as *resistant*, I believe that this is an improper use of the term, and that we are dealing here with a need to reconcile true no's—hence the term "negotiation" for this kind of exchange. Another example of where no's are processed, as opposed to being resistance exchanges, is in any management group decision-making setting where the participants see themselves as being roughly equal in power or status. Since this does not occur often, many managers experience interactions with presumed peers as replete with resistance, and not as negotiations around no's.

Recipients of "no" statements may not like to receive this reaction, but they will usually experience it as having much more focus and clarity than what they perceive to be manifestations of resistance—generally seen as poorly defined or ill-structured statements. Looking at resistance in this way helps us to understand why so many consultants emphasize participation and empowerment in their organization development efforts; they value organizations where the no's are expressed and dealt with in a healthy, direct way, and potential for resistance is minimized. But until such ideals are the norm, power differentials will continue to exist and those with less power will use indirect no's if they do not readily accept influence or do what others want them to do. Anyone who doubts this needs only to look at or recall a child saying "no" to a parent. Adults rarely receive such a negative statement as a healthy reaction, but rather as misguided or, worse yet, as a petulant answer. Among adults, however, a conscious choice to say "no" in a responsive way is a mature, healthy reaction.

From this argument we can see that managers have some special problems in how their goal orientation may create resistance in others. If we look at how managers define their jobs, we see responsibility for initiating change as one of the major tasks. At any given level of hierarchy, a manager does not expect that those who are subordinate to that level will initiate change, and when subordinates do so, they generally have a hard time of it. In this we realize that power differentials and the manifestation of resistance work in both an upward and downward direction: "As manager, I reserve the right to resist your attempts to influence me, and I reserve the right to try to overcome your resistance to my attempts to influence you." If such a manager recognizes his or her positional power as vested authority, rather than divine right, opposition is less likely to be labeled as being bad. However, if one's self-concept as a manager or holder of authority can only be validated through the full attainment of agreement with one's goals or methods, failure of others to join up in this way will be seen as resistance and considered disruptive behavior. Thus the more that managers fail to see that authority is distributed in all parts of any system, the more likely they are to overinvest in specific outcomes of an influence process. They do not see that any time a direction is chosen by one part of the authority system, it invites both *joining* and *op-*

posing forces from other parts. Western managers, particularly Americans, have a hard time with this because of cultural values around individual responsibility and accountability. The more collective culture of the Japanese manager lessens the potential for resistance by employing a cautious, feeling-out process of all concerned with an issue, avoiding firm, open stances attributed to any single individual. As Pascale (1978) has pointed out, the Japanese are much more able to accept ambiguity as a normal state of affairs and to see obstacles to any goal as inevitable. This accounts for their ability to take a great deal of time in making a decision and to avoid premature pushes for action.

AWARENESS PROCESS AND RESISTANCE

From the Gestalt perspective, if one were to achieve full awareness about one's feelings and thoughts concerning perceived pressure to change, the result would be *ambivalence*. If one fully encountered all of the internal and external reality in the situation, forces for both joining with the proposal and opposing it would be felt. And while the perceived, more conscious forces might be larger on the side of opposition at any given moment, the Gestalt perspective assumes that some part of the person is for the proposal, and that there is no such thing as an all-or-nothing position. Some aspect of the proposal may be readily acceptable, while another aspect is seen as abhorrent. One may be for an idea or method but reluctant to face a change in one's own behavior in order to actualize it. Many people are afraid of novelty in certain areas of their life, but they also have some small degree of fascination with the new or exotic. If the goal is to understand one's reaction fully, to achieve full awareness about it, then working with these differences or opposites becomes a powerful tool, as any therapist experienced in working with clients around polarities knows. One of Fritz Perls' great insights was to take Friedlander's concept of creative indifference and apply it to the realm of psychotherapy. This theory states that every event is related to a zero point, out of which opposites are differentiated. As Perls (1947) expressed it:

> These opposites show in their specific context a great affinity to each other. By remaining alert in the centre, we can acquire a creative ability of seeing both sides of an occurrence and completing an incomplete half.

If we apply this to the experience of resistance, we come to the conclusion that what we label as resistance in others is not just a process of opposition. It is a complex experience with many aspects, only some of which are figural at the moment for both the resister and the perceiver of resistance. While this is a subtle point, and may seem to some a matter of semantics, this orienting principle is the key to any possibiilty of working with resistance by either managers or consultants. In fact, I propose that the term "resistance" be deleted from our vocabulary because it has come to mean opposition or a one-sided reaction. Instead it will be much better to refer to any instance where one or more persons do not seem to be "joining" as a manifestation of *multidirected energy*. This term conveys the notion of multiple forces or desires, not all of which support each other, and many of which pull in different directions. It represents more accurately than does the concept of resistance the experience of both individuals and groups in reacting to the initiation of change. In Chapter 2, the Interactive Cycles that lack a common "joining" point (Figures 2–4, 2–7) are examples of *multidirected energy*.

If the manifestation we have been calling resistance is now seen as multidirected energy, it helps us to understand its dynamic nature in other ways. For example, we can look at it in terms of being a flexible rather than a fixed phenomenon, as being an expression of a moment in time in a process that may just be beginning. Perhaps it is the first reaction to the change, not necessarily the last. For many people it may be that, "I don't know what I want, I haven't said anything yet," or it may be that some need to say "no" before they can say "yes." At any rate, this kind of thinking seems more hopeful for effectively dealing with the situation than focusing solely on the negative, nonjoining aspects. This does not mean that it will be easy to change the reaction, but it does mean that engagement in a process is required rather than acceptance of a fixed position.

Up to this point, the focus has been largely on the situation between a manager and others who may be showing resistance. This is the case whenever one person decides to influence others to do something. What about the situation in which a consultant is asked to help a work system and experiences "resistance" to the helping effort? This may look as if a different focus is required, but I believe that exactly the same reasoning is useful: behind the seemingly positive request for help—a move by the initiator(s) to "join"—lies ambivalence. In fact, it was exactly this insight that led Freud to develop the concept of resistance, and to design psychoanalysis as a method of dealing with it. Every importance psychoanalytic theorist since Freud has had something to say about this, using the term "conflict" more often than that of "ambivalence" to describe this multidirected energy, but essentially talking about an occurrence very similar to that experienced by consultants. Table 8-1 shows how Karl Menninger (1958) portrayed this in his classic work on psychoanalytic technique. While some of the specifics do not seem relevant to the consulting situation, it is relatively easy to do a similar analysis of ambivalence, or conflicting forces, in this setting. For example:

1. The client wants the consultant to do a good job of assessment, but does not want too many people bothered by requests for information, or does not want to be shamed or embarrassed by what might be revealed.
2. The client knows that change takes time and is not easy to bring about, but becomes annoyed when the consultant makes a proposal that cannot be implemented quickly.
3. The client is looking for new ways of doing things, but has all sorts of reasons why different things will not work.
4. The client likes the advice received, but receives advice from others that is different and also plausible.
5. The client accepts a report from the consultant, but it is not implemented, or it is implemented with significant changes by the client that are seen as dysfunctional by the consultant.

This list can be expanded, but the point is made: Behind every request for consulting services—no matter how positive and strong the request—there lies an ambivalent client. Again we see

Table 8-1. A Psychoanalytic Model of Ambivalence in the Helping Relationship: A Way of Looking at "Multidirected Energy"

Diagrammatic Recapitulation of Resistance

The forces working against the process of recovery in psychoanalytic therapy may be paired at various levels with the positive efforts they oppose, thus:

The patient wants to get help from the analyst, *but* it is costly, time-consuming, strange, somewhat frightening, etc.

The patient wants to cooperate, follow instructions, "tell all," etc. *but* it causes humiliation, shame, embarrassment, etc.

The patient wants love from the analyst, whomever he or she represents, *but* obtaining love is dangerous, uncertain, and costly.

The patient feels resentful toward the analyst for his or her silence and passivity and would like to tell the analyst so, *but* the consequences might be unpleasant, and even dangerous.

The patient responds to the encouragement of the analyst and the analytic situation to let himself or herself go to some extent, *but* this offends his self-esteem, "seems so silly," unbecoming, indecorous, "and probably futile."

The patient is tempted to reveal repressed memories and suppressed fantasies, *but* "Surely, that can't be so," "It cannot have been I!"

The patient tries to get a clearer picture of long-buried unconscious strivings, *but* "It may be too horrible! I can't look. . . ."

The patient finally sees glimpses of how he or she has been misled by illusions and hatreds; sees "The Better Way," or at least a better way, a more intelligent and realistic choice, *but* "I'm so used to my muddlings and misery; dare I make a shift? Do I really want to give it up? And how can I be sure?"

The patient gradually gives up dependence upon analysis and the analyst and any unrealistic expectations of them; the patient is almost able to handle life problems alone, and more expediently, *but* "Am I really ready? Might I not fail? Might I not relapse?"

the unfolding of a dialectic that seems so pervasive that it may well be the natural order of things in all influence exchanges among mature, healthy adults. Perhaps it is more unnatural and unhealthy to absorb outside help unquestioningly—to introject, in Gestalt terms—than it is to resist. In supervising students doing consulting assignments, I push them to examine their joy at having little or no resistance from the client system; it does not seem natural to me if they cannot sense ambivalence or multidirected energy somewhere in the system.

DEALING WITH RESISTANCE

We come, then, to looking at how to deal with resistance. The place to start is to assume that it is a healthy, self-regulating manifestation that must be respected as such by the consultant. If this is done, it leads to strategies and tactics for working with the resistance as opposed to trying to overcome it or annihilate it. As indicated earlier, attempting to overpower, avoid, or eliminate it does not allow full awareness of the experience by either the initiator or the resisters. This is patronizing behavior and is not respectful of the integrity of either party. To "leap over" the resistance is to avoid the possibility of real insight or growth, and it precludes full ownership of the resistance. Even if the oppositional forces are thus dissipated, the outcome is compliance, which may be alright in a coercive setting but is not a good, long-term, problem-solving, or educational model for the system involved.

On a more positive note, the paradoxical theory of change—the basis of the Gestalt approach to change—supports staying with the resistance as a tactical matter. This theory states that a person or system cannot move from one state of being to another until the present state is fully experienced and accepted. Working from this premise leads to efforts to heighten the present state: all the thoughts and feelings associated with it need to be articulated and assimilated. If the "no" or opposing side is more figural, this is to be respected, attended to, and worked with first in order to enlarge the awareness and ownership of the opposer and the initiator. Then, and only then, is there a possibility that any of the joining forces in the multidirected energy can be allowed expression, attention, and consideration.

In psychotherapy this process is sometimes referred to as the working-through process. Another way of putting it is to say that the objections to doing something new may have to be fully examined before there can be full examination of the reasons for doing it. For managers this means first soliciting and listening to all the objections that people have to it before working on all the reasons why a proposed change might be desirable. This cannot be done without momentarily holding in abeyance investment in achieving the outcome as proposed. Pushing for the outcome will only solidify the resistance by not allowing room for opposing forces to be balanced with joining forces. The accountability-oriented, results-driven manager will have a hard time accepting this notion, but there is no other way to avoid the enlargement of the resistance that will follow from continued assaults on the integrity or self-esteem of the targets of change.

EXAMPLES OF HOW TO DEAL WITH MULTIDIRECTIONAL ENERGY

Case One

> In conducting educational interventions, such as a two- or three-day workshop on a given topic, it is quite common to find that many of the participants do not wish to be there. Some have mild objections; others say little or nothing and take part without showing overt dissatisfaction. However, quite frequently there is an individual who is outspoken in expressing that he or she is not pleased about being at the event and would prefer not to be an active participant. (This phenomenon tends to occur where a human resource manager or a superior of the person makes the nomination for attendance at either a company-run or public seminar.) My standard reaction to this is to deal with it as soon as the person makes it public, and to make it clear to that person that I am in sympathy with his or her feelings. In talking to the entire group,

I will address the participant's reluctance as pointedly as possible.

I would not want to be at a program that did not interest me. I assume that you came because you were not able to decline attendance or that you were not clear what the program entailed. At any rate, I hope you will stay and not participate any more than you feel is comfortable for you. You can change your mind at any time; sometime later in the program I may check with you about this, but otherwise, it is fine with me if you do not say anything.

I then turn to the entire group and ask them if it is alright with them if that person remains inactive. I generally get universal agreement that this is acceptable.

Sometimes, the reluctant participant does not stay out of it to the end and I make sure to check a couple of times to see what he or she is experiencing. However, more often, the person will elect to enter the program someplace along the way, generally when some kind of feedback exercise is involved. By remaining more or less on the sideline, this person has become a perceptive observer of much that is happening, and by allowing room for free choice of entry, the group receives useful, sometimes brilliant observations. Moreover, both the reluctant and the active participant gain real respect for the stance of the other, and both have increased respect for the tolerance of the active participants to accept differences and, apparently, deviant behavior. There has been some learning about empowerment as well as about the subject matter of the workshop. I have provided a demonstration of how multidirected energy can be respected, and of how awareness can be enlarged and heightened so that some movement in the direction of joining may be possible later.

Case Two

In conducting a session of an inhouse management development program of a large corporation, I was faced with strong objections from a group of about 25 managers. Every concept or learning exercise was met with a negative reaction of some kind. The first day predicted a total disaster, and I felt as though I had been working with a"100-pound load on my back." In the middle of the afternoon, I put the preplanned schedule aside and confronted the group with my experience of them and the way the day had progressed. After some moments of avoidant responses from the group, to which I replied by pushing them further to "level" with me, I began to get straightforward comments from the group. They told me they were surprised that the corporation had designed this program, which did not meet any of their needs, and that they could not imagine it was well received by previous groups within the company. I tried to draw out every objection I could get from them. I asked them to tell me what would be more useful to them. Then I confronted them with the problem facing us: I had a contract to conduct the program and would be in breach of it if I stopped at that point: they had consented to attend when asked or told to do so, and would have to deal with their superiors if they left the program or otherwise prevented it from going on as planned. After considerable discussion we arrived at the following "contract": I would rearrange the second half of the last day to deal with a topic of interest to them and to help them prepare a statement for their superiors about what would be more helpful to them in future programs. Since I had planned for a program evaluation at the end, they would have their chance to send their reactions and advice about my program back to the people who had engaged me to design and conduct the program. We then quit for the day and came back for the remaining two days with a new understanding. They allowed me to "present my wares" and gave me feedback as to what was useful or not useful to them. At the end, I presided over a session in which the managers thought about and developed a useful input to their superiors about their perceived needs.

I cannot say that this experience turned out to be a huge success from the standpoint of what I wanted to teach. Some of the participants remained quiet, surly, or only moderately interested. However, if they had so much energy directed to things other than my curriculum, what could have been accomplished if I tried to work around their opposition or ambivalence? By responding to them, I helped them to take responsibility for their attitudes and behavior. I did get the attention of a significant number of people when I presented my material, and I was later able to say to the executives who engaged me for this program that I did present most of what was planned, but that I received negative reactions to this material and suggestions for what might be more useful. If the goal was to energize the client system, we were reasonably successful in enlarging awareness in the area of management development—even though it was at the expense of my comfort level.

Case Three

A number of years ago I was engaged to do organization development in a company headed by two brothers who had inherited a business after the death of their father. During the first phase of this relationship, the older brother acted as president of the company, and the work involved resolving differences in business objectives between him and the younger brother. I also helped to reorganize and build the management staff required to keep up with a growing business. All of the top-level managers went to a stranger sensitivity training program while the other work progressed. After two years or so on this track, the older brother became ill and was away from the job for about seven months. In his absence, the younger brother assumed the presidency—by agreement between the two of them—and continued to use my services in building the organization. One of the things he decided was to change the management style from a loosely organized consultative style to participative management. He felt that the managers were not speaking up enough in meetings and that they needed more encouragement to do so, and to develop more of a sense of ownership and involvement in the company. To aid in this, we began a series of weekly staff meetings in which I was to act as process consultant. In addition, a quarterly two-day retreat was scheduled for team-building purposes.

At the start of the management meetings, most of the managers were reluctant to speak freely. The president—a mild-mannered man who generally avoided conflict and did little to create it—was frustrated by this but was patient and continued to try to foster a welcoming atmosphere. I contributed with numerous interventions in which people were asked for their responses to issues affecting them, and by supporting the president's wish for greater participation. After some months of this process, people did begin to open up, expressing more ideas and deeper feelings as we discussed business problems. At one session, several managers expressed some criticism of the president, particularly around his reluctance to act more aggressively in certain situations. As this negative feedback unfolded, the president became uneasy and defensive, and tried to present rational reasons to support his behavior. After the meeting he took me aside and said: "What is the matter with you? I asked you to help me get more participation, not to support attacks on me." I told him that I was doing what I thought he had asked me to do, namely, to encourage people to be more open in articulating their ideas. I asked him to tell me more about his feelings and thoughts as he heard the negative feedback (which, incidentally, seemed only mildly negative from my perspective) and to let me know if he was concerned about continuing with our process.

Before continuing with a discussion of how I dealt further with this situation, it is important to realize that this is a classic case of the client who seeks help and then behaves in a "resistant" manner as the helping process unfolds. In the Gestalt framework, we refer to this as ambivalence and, as stated earlier, see it as a natural, not necessarily unhealthy condition. One way to look at this situation is to assume that the president decided on intellectual grounds that a more participative management style was right for him and his subordinates. At the moment he made this decision, any doubts or concerns he may have had were minor or dormant in his consciousness. It was not until he had more information—the data of his growing awareness as we worked to achieve participation—that his negative feelings emerged. A reasonable assumption here is that the data energized his emotional side, a much more difficult arena for him. It was not until then that the basic issue became apparent, though he did not seem to realize this when he expressed his discomfort to me. If we look at this entire sequence in the light of the Cycle of Experience, we can say that the president started with some awareness that mobilized him into action. But the ensuing contact was more than he could easily handle at that point.

To understand my approach to this situation, it will help to look at one important factor to consider when doing team building with hierarchically related managers. This has to do with "face saving," and an underlying fear of those at the highest levels in the group that they might be seen as vulnerable or less than fully competent in the eyes of subordinates. While lower-level managers in these settings often express concern that it might be held against them if they speak too freely, this assumption has been shown time and time again to have much less strength than the unspoken fears of the senior managers. For this reason it seemed dysfunctional to me to ask the president to state his feelings to the group. Even without this guideline, I had an additional cue in that he mentioned his concerns to me privately. I had to assume that he was not ready at that moment to speak freely about his feelings to the group. (Note that this is exactly the symptom he had identified as the problem of his managers.)

With the above in mind, I proposed to the president that he and I hold some private sessions to take a look at what was happening. In this way he could express himself with somewhat less concern for "face saving" and we could work at the awareness level for a while. Before the next meeting, we held three two-hour sessions for this purpose. My objective was not to make sure that he was ready to continue the participative format; it was to help him to explore his conflicting sides after which he could decide whether to handle the discomfort or not to proceed. My main purpose was to examine his objections to sharing his feelings. In helping him to examine his assumptions and fears—including that of "face saving," as well as the nature of his emotions—he began to understand himself a little better. This enabled us to look at some ways in which it was possible for him to share his feelings about being criticized. He decided that he could do this if criticism occurred again, and we resumed the meetings. This choice was not made without some trepidation on his part, nor did it result in an easy time for him in some later sessions. However, as he began to loosen up somewhat himself, so did his subordinate managers.

IMPLICATIONS

The major implication of the above is that the task of the consultant is *to help the client system deal with its multidirected energies*. As stated earlier, change in the behavior of the client is an option of the client, and is not a primary task of intervention. But helping people to see the full meaning of their joining and opposing forces around any work-system issue is perhaps *the* primary function of a consultant when change and resistance to change is being considered.

Since most objectives for which organization consultants are hired are positive or desirable, there is a built-in tendency for consultants to support movement toward these goals. This is not simply a question of being paid for the work; it is a function of at least broadly similar values. Managers almost unwittingly set up the use of driving forces to get the targets of their change efforts to move toward a desired state. However, as Lewin's work in force-field analysis and the Gestalt approach to heightening awareness have taught us, joining can be obtained through attending to the restraining forces. This means that significant movement, or learning that movement is not possible at a given time, will come from consultant effort to bring out the objections to joining and sharpen them for all concerned. I call this "taking a bath in the resistance together with the client." After such immersion it may be more useful to use persuasion or more aggressive driving forces to support movement when the client system is ready to move. In an organizational setting involving a number of people, this requires making room for the "opposition" so that it has at least equal, if not more, time to become known to all concerned.

REFERENCES

Coch, L., and French, J.R.P. "Overcoming resistance to change." In D. Cartwright, and A. Zander (eds.), *Group Dynamics: Research and Theory.* Evanston, Ill.: Row, Peterson, 1960.

Klein, D. "Some notes on the dynamics of resistance to change: The defender role." In Bennis, Benne, et al. (eds.), *The Planning of Change* (3rd edi.), 1976.

Kotter, J.P., and Schlesinger, L.A. "Choosing strategies for change," *Harvard Business Review,* March-April, 1979, pp. 106–114.

Lawrence, P.R. "How to deal with resistance to change," *Harvard Businss Review,* January–February, 1969.

Lewin, K. *Field Theory in Social Science.* New York: Harper & Co., 1951.

Menninger, K. *Theory of Psychoanalytic Technique.* New York: Basic Books, 1958.

Pascale, R.T. "Zen and the art of management," *Harvard Business Review,* March–April, 1978.

Perls, F.S. *Ego, Hunger and Aggression.* New York: Random House, 1947.

Polster, E., and Polster, M. *Gestalt Therapy Integrated.* New York: Brunner/Mazel, 1973.

9
Developing Relationships with Clients: Organization Consulting as Contrasted with Psychotherapy*

This chapter deals with some issues that are not unique to a Gestalt perspective, but for which understanding is enhanced by the concepts of awareness and presence. The issues relate to the expectations that clients and consultants have of each other with regard to the structure and quality of their relationships. This includes questions of the ground rules for the work, the definition of who is the client, role clarification for each party, and ways of dealing with multidirected energy within the client–consultant unit. As a means of enhancing our understanding of these factors, it is useful to contrast the way they appear in organization consulting with how they are manifested in the psychotherapeutic relationship. From this comparison we can draw some important implications for the work of the consultant.

Among the issues in question, the definition of who is the client is a prime example. This is a very complex issue in organization consulting, and finds its parallel in psychotherapy with couples and families. (In the case of individual therapy, there are

*The ideas expressed in this chapter grew out of several conversations with Sonia M. Nevis and Elaine Kepner.

often questions as to whether the therapist is dealing with the "right" client, but most therapists would agree that, until a change is made, the person they are seeing is the client.) In organization consulting, one does not consult with "the firm" even in those instances where large-scale change is the goal and the work is done solely with senior management or the board of directors. One deals with parts, units, and levels of an organization, often shifting the focus of attention as the work proceeds over time. Moreover, in many cases senior management seeks out or approves the use of consulting help but then delegates the coordination or direction of the work to lower levels of management. In such instances there are multiple constituencies, and the consultant must negotiate a contract with each of the client systems. In fact, it may be useful to view the entire consulting experience as a continuous series of such negotiations, especially when the gathering of data and the implementation of changes involve significant numbers of people at all levels of the organization. Furthermore, changes within the defined client system may have bothersome or negative effects on surrounding or adjacent parts of the organization. The responsible consultant tries to anticipate and deal with these consequences, but frequently has no relationship or "contract" with the bordering units. The consultant may then attempt to make this issue a task for the defined client system to handle, but even this obvious move brings into focus once again the question of who is the client.

Our two basic aspects of the Gestalt approach are helpful in guiding the consultant's response to these problems.

1. *The Interactive Cycle of Experience.* Each time a consultant begins to relate to another part of the organization, new figural elements are involved and a new Cycle is initiated out of this awareness by the consultant. A new entry and assessment phase may be called for, even if the work is in what might be considered the intervention or implementation phase. The need for additional, new work at the awareness and energy (joining) levels may require a momentary halt or a redirection of what is happening at the action level. Thus one might not stop a project simply because an adjacent unit objected to what the defined client unit was doing, but it is hard to imagine that a consultant would proceed without bringing

this awareness into the immediate foreground of the client.

2. *Presence*. While there may be some useful guidelines as to tactics for dealing with changing and/or multiple client constituencies, the success of the consultant in negotiating the required relationships will depend largely on consultant presence. This means that the consultant must be interesting enough to gain the attention of the newcomers long enough to see if a useful contract can be developed. Even when people may be "ordered" to cooperate by their superiors—in fact, especially in such instances—the consultant must use the force of presence to create compelling interest in the endeavor. Without this, the ambivalence around participating may become one-sided and oppositional in its weight. The useful aspects of multidirected energy may be lost to both consultant and client because of the failure to bring into full public view the nature of the opposing forces.

This point is amply illustrated by one example of a common experience in dealing with reluctant or nonvoluntary client systems. In this instance several managers who became part of an organization development effort initiated at a higher level were distrustful of the consultants, and they behaved in a withdrawn or mildly teasing way through several meetings. The two consultants (of whom I was one) were aware of this, but confined their responses to occasional inquiries as to whether these managers wanted to add anything to the discussion. Other than this, we focused our efforts on the work at hand, which was task oriented around an agenda that some of the managers in the group helped to develop. We dealt with the group as a whole, doing what I call "displaying our wares." At the end of a planning session in which a significant amount of time was devoted to process observations by the consultants, one of these managers said: "I've been watching you consultants for some time now, and I must say that you are the only people I have seen who get paid for saying what's on your mind, and for telling people just what you think of them!" The other manager, a close friend of the first, nodded his head in agreement with this statement. While the statement was not quite a true description of what we were doing, it let us know that we were becoming interesting to these managers. We encouraged them to say more about their observations and how they felt about what we were doing. We did not get much by way of response to our encouragement, but we felt that this indication of their interest in us provided a beginning for negotiations concerning the nature of their participation in the project.

DIFFERENCES BETWEEN CONSULTING AND PSYCHOTHERAPY

There are other important relationship issues, and they can be highlighted by a comparison of the practice of organization consulting with that of psychotherapy. The differences between the two modes are most keenly experienced by those who have been trained in one mode and then begin to work in the other. An examination of the modes in relation to such professional role transitions is illuminating.

It is now quite common for clinically trained helping professionals to engage in organization consulting at some time in their career. For some this work is an adjunct to a career of primarily therapeutic work; for others the appeal of doing systems consulting has led to significant changes in career focus. While this phenomenon appears to be growing, it is not a new one. Indeed, in the early days of organization consulting by professionals with a human relations orientation, the modal practitioner was one who began his or her training in clinical or educational psychology. Skills in diagnostic testing, interviewing, and counseling were considered relevant and transferable to human problems in an organizational setting. Some of the now-senior people in the field of organization development can point to a history of education and practice in such varied fields as Freudian psychoanalysis, Rogerian nondirective counseling, Gestalt therapy, and Skinnerian-oriented behavior modification.

A parallel development over the past 30 years or so has been a trend in the opposite direction. That is to say, many people who came to organization consulting from a management career or a work system perspective, rather than from a clinical occupation, have sought training in therapeutic-related skills and concepts in order to become more effective in working one on one and at the small-group level in organization settings. A small number of these people now conduct some counseling or psychotherapy as part of their practice.

In observing friends, colleagues, and students make these transitions, and in being asked by many clinically trained people about opportunities, satisfactions, and problems in doing consulting work, I have come better to appreciate the similarities and differences in the two areas of work. While both the therapist and consultant derive much power from the marginal role they play as disturbers of boundaries; the nature of the interaction with clients, the way contracts are developed, and the like, vary significantly in the two modes. One of the key differences became clear to me some 30 years ago when I was a therapy client at the same time that I was developing an organization consulting firm. As a client it seemed that I devoted a great deal of concern and time to gaining the approval of my therapist. I often felt—more in retrospect than in any given therapy session—that I was trying both to learn how to be a happier person and to have the therapist like me. In the consulting setting, what struck me was the frequency with which members of the client organization seemed to be waiting for me to display my wares and to prove that I, the "therapist/consultant," had something to offer. In this case it was as though I had to earn their approval, a reversal of my experience in the client–therapist interaction. While therapy clients certainly evaluate and criticize their therapists, organizational client groups do not easily see themselves as entering into a contract modeled along the lines of interdependent learning, or dependent emotional relationships, such as is the core of psychotherapy. In the therapeutic realm, the closest parallel to the organizational setting is in family therapy, where one member of a family often decides that this is a good thing to do and then tries to convince the others to be part of the endeavor. This results in a need for the therapist to display wares and gain "approval" similar to that noted in organizational settings. The power of presence is particularly important in determining how wares are displayed.

In discussing this with Sonia Nevis, who is a psychotherapist, I noted another significant difference. It occurred to me that in therapy settings there is much physical and mental moving around by clients and a more waiting, seemingly stationary stance by the therapist. We refer to the position of the therapist with the metaphor "working by sitting down." By contrast, many organization consultants experience that their work not only involves formal presentations, but a generally more active physical and mental movement to display wares to a more "passive" client. This mode of work may be referred to as "working by standing up." Those who work in the human resources field will note the similarity of this concept to a frequent comment of consultants that one of their most common interventions is "stand-up training."

In looking at these two modes side by side, it appears that management-oriented consultants seeking to learn therapeutic skills wish to incorporate more use of the "sitting down" approach into their work, and clinically trained people moving into organization consulting want to learn how to work by "standing up." The Gestalt orientation is particularly helpful in understanding and managing the work in both modes. An appreciation of the Cycle of Experience orients one to the need to be careful and thorough at the awareness level, so that contextual and contracting factors are highlighted before moving into energy-mobilizing and contact-enhancing interventions. Moreover, as will become clear, presence becomes a critical factor in how well the practitioner navigates through each of these modes.

Before looking more systematically at the differences between "working by sitting down" and "working by standing up," it may be useful to look at a key similarity of psychotherapy and consultation. Both are based on the development and continual refinement of a contract between two parties in which it is presumed that one side wants to move to a better state of functioning and being, and that the other party possesses some skills or values that can enable the first party to do this. It may be assumed by the helping party that he or she might also learn and grow in this process, but this is a secondary feature to that of the hiring party gaining benefit from the services provided. Whether made explicit or not, all therapy or consultation rests on some model of the educational process. Learning is the central process at issue in both endeavors. This includes both the heightening of awareness and the development of skills.

STRUCTURAL ASPECTS OF PSYCHOTHERAPY AND CONSULTING

There is a great deal of literature about therapy and consultation as education, mostly focusing on theories and problems of adult learning. For the present purpose, the focus is more on understanding the significant structural and process issues involved in the development of an educational contract. This is critical to both modes. At one extreme, for example, there is a basically voluntary act in which an individual or couple seeks out a therapist/teacher and buys a "course" of short- or long-term duration. At the other, some member of an organization engages a "teacher" and offers the remainder of the group as "students," with all degrees of voluntarism on their part. Working in both modes can be best understood through elaboration of such differences and their implications. In studying these factors and others, it is important to keep in mind that these structural events have profound consequences for the learning experience.

We can now look at some of the differences in how the educational endeavor is structured in the two settings. To begin with, organization consultation by definition involves work with more than one individual. While the work is often supported by individual counseling, more typically one-on-one interactions take place largely between the consultant and the gatekeeping member(s) of the organization—the person(s) who brought the consultant into the organization. These interactions include both developmental counseling by the consultant and politically oriented strategizing around how the consulting work can best be developed to serve the needs of the organization. Certainly this is quite different from what takes place in most therapy sessions, where therapists may give advice but strive to avoid any kind of preferential alliance with some client members in relation to other members in the client group. The fundamental issue here is that successful systems consulting requires ownership of the endeavor by all involved, and that all members of the group defined as the client system are not at the same place with respect to a need for change or readiness to undertake a learning project. While this occurs quite frequently in family therapy, it is a critical issue in almost all organizational intervention based on process consultation models. Indeed, it is the core of the question: "Who is the client?"

The situation is different in the case of psychotherapy, especially with individuals. In this situation, an individual seeks out a particular therapist with whom he or she wishes to work. This may be done through a referral process, or through reputation or acquaintanceship of some form, but it is the culmination of conscious, voluntary desire to work with a given "teacher." And, unlike the case of organization consulting, where an organization makes payment for services rendered, the person seeking help generally makes direct, personal payment to the therapist. Even with third-party payments to therapists, there is little confusion as to whom the client is and where ownership of the enterprise resides. A consultant may work with just one or two individuals in an organization, but it is questionable that this can be called organization consulting. Perhaps it might be better to designate this work as organizationally sponsored individual counseling. This would make it clearer to the consultant that the work is mainly work by "sitting down." The impact of this on significant others in the organization must be considered, but there is no implicit or explicit understanding that an organization change project is under way.

There are many other important differences in the mode of work. There is an almost precious quality to the therapeutic relationship, in which intimacy and high, personal contact between therapist and client are central to the work. On the organizational side, intimacy issues become quite complicated: the consultant needs to use high-contact means in order to "grab" the interest of the client system, but essentially the task is to promote good contact among members of the client system. In organization consulting intimacy might be better defined as attraction based on respect for the professional stance and competence of all parties. Though some consultants do indeed become very close to some members of the client system—particularly with their gatekeepers or key contacts—they are presumably hired to work with the entire system and not to bond too closely with particular members. Much of the value of a consultant to an organization lies in the skill possessed by that person to promote better contact among members of the system, not with the consultant. Promotion of high personal contact with the consultant would appear to be most useful as a means of preparing individuals to work better with each other. Third-party intervention is an excellent example of where the role of the consultant is more like that of a stage manager than that of an actor. Yet, if the consultant is too aloof or distant, impact or opportunity for influence may be diminished. The therapist must deal with a similar problem, trying not to become too personally involved or confluent with the client, but recognizing that much of the growth of the client will come through intense interaction with the therapist. The way in which presence is manifested may be differentially useful in this regard. Thus presence that emphasizes more of an explicit, clinical mode may be more acceptable to industrial organizations than a more mysterious, contactful mode.

Related to this is the private versus public nature of the modes, and the satisfaction or frustration that each setting can bring. In psychotherapy the room in which the work is performed is an inner sanctum, and the "rules of the game" are very much dictated by the therapist once the client enters that space. This is not simply an issue of control, but one that relates to the nature of the language, mannerisms, and idiosyncracies of the therapist. The work is carried out on a very private stage, with the therapist being both actor and director. In the organizational setting, the consultant may have great freedom as to ground rules—indeed, the need to establish presence and uniqueness is critical to the work—but the consultant works on the territory of the client organization most of the time and is constantly in a negotiating position as to what the rules of the game will be and what behavior is possible. For example, I hate doing team-development sessions in hotel or motel settings, but many clients see nothing wrong with doing the work in large convention centers or central city hotels. Even more critical here is the need to negotiate differences around my desired assessment and intervention procedures and those acceptable to the client. Again, this issue is not just that of being true to one's style; it is one of arranging the important structures and settings for the work. An effective consultant will do well at these negotiations, knowing that each issue provides an opportunity to enhance his or her presence, and that these are just some of the many key events performed in more or less public group settings when one engages in organization consulting.

Table 9-1 summarizes these points and some related differences in the modes of "sitting down" and "standing up." While much of this will appear obvious to those who are experienced practitioners in these domains, these issues are often ignored by both therapists and consultants, or placed in a secondary position to that of dealing with the content of presenting problems or symptoms. The privately oriented therapist may misperceive what is involved in performing on a stage with a critical audience in the room. Having to negotiate rules of work may be seen as an annoyance by a therapist, rather than as an important learning issue. On the other hand, the consultant who enjoys operating in an arena larger than the private room may have significant difficulty in achieving good one-to-one contacts when this is essential to the work. Failing to recognize the anxiety-producing nature of doing unsupported work in someone else's territory may lead to dysfunctional intimacy with those members of the client group most sympathetic to the values of the consultant. An understanding of these factors is critical to the success of the work and leads to some important implications.

IMPLICATIONS

One implication is that the organization consultant has a more difficult task than the therapist with regard to the issue of displaying wares and resolution of the approval issue. A therapist may sit with a client and wait for relatively long periods of time for something to happen, and this may be considered good therapist technique. In the consulting setting, such behavior is very likely to lead to discomfort and a deteriorating relationship if the consultant does not respond to the inevitable irritation of the client system. It takes the highest form of consulting art to handle these moments in a respectful (to the client) and yet compelling way. It is at this time that presence of

Table 9-1. Differences in "Working by Sitting Down" and "Working by Standing Up"

"Sitting Down" (Voluntary Psychotherapy Model)	*"Standing Up" (Organization Consulting Model)*
Individuals usually seek out and choose therapist; pay therapist personally; the relationship is one on one.	Someone in system seeks out and engages consultant for the system; consultant paid by the organization.
Works on therapist's territory; usual supports and rules of therapist prevail.	Work on client's territory, often without usual supports; usually must negotiate the "rules of the game."
Mostly private events; therapist has low public visibility.	Public events prevail; evaluated by many people and have a more public reputation.
Person with whom therapist is working wants something from therapist	Often great variability in client members as to what they want from consultant, or as to what consultant has to offer.
Client's values generally close to those of the therapist	Person(s) hiring consultant (gatekeepers) may be only ones in system with values similar to consultant's.
Client is seen as owning problem, even if confused as to its nature.	Not clear as to what the problem is and who owns it.
Emphasizes high interpersonal contact between therapist and client; personal vibrations between two are critical.	Consultant works to promote contact among parts of the system through facilitative behavior.
Client puts a lot of effort into proving himself or herself to the therapist	Clients expect the consultant to prove himself or herself to them.

the consultant will be most critical to the success of the relationship. In this setting one must display his or her wares before asking too much of the client, but this does not indicate what to exhibit and how to do it. Should conceptual and/or experiential material be introduced early? Should truly gripping interpersonal high-contact interventions be employed early? Or, backing up a bit, should the consultant try to obtain early feedback from the client system as to how he or she is being perceived? However one chooses to handle the early stages of relationship building, I am convinced that the most useful stance is one in which simple, clear display of wares is given freely, but an aura of some mysticism is also established in the process. A "performance" must be presented, but it may be best to limit it to a short, exciting prologue of acts to follow. If one is highly rational and organized, there may not be enough mystery to hold attention long enough to be able to stage final scenes. If there is too much mystery or ambiguity, clients may experience discomfort or, worse yet, begin to project onto or attribute to the consultant characteristics of softness or incompetence. Without some aura of the unknown that intrigues but does not threaten, it may be hard to negotiate for effective ground rules. This may well be an argument against too much demystification of the consultation process. Those working primarily from a clinical orientation tend to underestimate the importance of dealing effectively with the beginnings of organizational work (unless they are well-trained family systems therapists). Those coming out of a management perspective tend to be much too rational and intervention oriented at the beginning, failing to develop enough interest in explorations of a more non-linear nature.

The second implication is that family therapy and organization consulting have much in common when the role of the intervenor is considered. If the individually trained practitioner is to be successful in working at the system level, the skills of the organization consultant must be blended with those of the therapist. Modern family system theorists work from such a perspective. Their approaches treat presenting problems or symptoms as of secondary importance, they focus on structural issues in the client–therapist relationship and on the family's process as a system. Their aim is to teach the system skills for more effective functioning as an organization. The therapist who does not appreciate the centrality of questions such as ownership, definition of who the client is, and what useful contact is, may achieve developmental movement through useful work with each of the individual members but will fail to improve the organization. Incidentally, family system theorists have extremely illuminating insights and perspectives of use to the organization consultant; they are often quite creative in combining the best features of the "sitting down" and the "standing up" approaches.

The third implication to be drawn from this comparison is that Gestalt therapy and related high-contact, experiential methods have much to offer the organization consultant when used appropriately. Though system level intervention means consideration of the system as a work unit—with focus on structural, process, and output variables—getting the client to examine these depends upon how interesting or compelling the consultant is in the contact made with the client. Presence and the use of self are critical and represent the highest order of skill needed for this work, perhaps more so than familiarity with the technology of organization development. On the other hand, a lack of appreciation for the basic, normative methods and procedures that give organizational life its special qualities can result in consultant presence seen as having too much verve or charisma, or in some other way as irrelevant. It is the setting of the work that defines the range of useful consultant presence, and Gestalt therapy is one approach to the helping relationship that teaches its practitioners how to make use of self in appropriately impactful ways. When combined with appreciation for the ways of "working by standing up," consultants can enhance their potency in relationships with client systems.

A further implication is that institutionally directed psychotherapy is in many ways similar to nonvoluntary client participation in organization consulting projects. When a court or other legal entity coerces someone to engage in therapy, the designated client is in the same position as the member of a working group who is forced to take part in a program for which he or she has not asked. In this instance the therapist is faced with the task of proving himself or herself, just as is the organization consultant in settings of nonvoluntary participants. A major difference between the two settings is that organization members frequently draw upon their feelings of belonging to the organization ("good soldier syndrome") and join into the enterprise eventually. In the institutional setting, the clients have had so many bad experiences with organizations in general that just being seen as an "agent" of an institution becomes an extremely harsh burden on the therapist. Anyone who has ever done counseling with hospital, clinic, or prison populations has felt this keenly. The only way to overcome this barrier is for the therapist to use every bit of energy and skill in the development of a presence that transcends the client–institution deadlock. The client must be drawn into an engrossing, compelling relationship so that the negative feelings toward the institution take second place to the almost heroic struggle being waged by therapist and client around the meaning and value of high contact. The implications of this are clear with regard to the nonvoluntary organizational settings: Unless the consultant can "grab" the participants and gain their attention, the relationship is likely to be a difficult one and prone to failure as a significant learning experience for the client.

ILLUMINATING CASES

Several examples will make the foregoing more concrete. These cases derive from a variety of settings.

Case One

> The president of a large urban college approached two of us at the Gestalt Institute of Cleveland concerning a program for his senior administrative staff and faculty department heads. After a couple of meetings with him and two key subordinates, it became clear that they conceived of a possible intervention in terms of staff development. That is, they were looking to skill development in a group setting as a means of improving cohesion and cooperation among the leaders of the organization. We were also led to believe that there was a strong difference of opinion among some of the faculty and administrators as to future direction for the college, including how to consolidate resources by possible elimination of some programs. We asked to start by doing an assessment of the perceptions of the needs and problems of the people to be involved and of their readiness to undertake a development effort. Since the college had a history of doing staff development, it made sense to us that this would be an acceptable way to enter the situation. The assessment was designed to make sure that the skill areas chosen were seen as important to a large number of the participants.

The project was introduced to the approximately 25 people involved at a meeting where we were given an opportunity to describe how we saw the situation and what our contribution might be. We asked for their cooperation in completing a confidential open-ended questionnaire and in taking part in small group interviews. In terms of the Cycle of Experience, and the issue of who the client was, this meeting may be seen as the completion of a unit of work with the president and his two key subordinates. This unit started with the initial meetings (awareness phase) and culminated in development and presentation of the assessment plan, first to the president, and then to the entire group. The meeting also represented the beginning of a new unit of work with a new client group. Introducing the project to the group was the first step in a process of negotiation with an expanded client system to determine its perceptions, needs, and readiness for developmental work.

The assessment process was accepted by the group after a discussion during which most participants expressed positive interest in doing some developmental work, though some key players said very little. We collected the questionnaires and conducted the interviews. What emerged from these inquiries was of little use with regard to identification of specific skill areas for development. There were some broad, cliche responses, such as "need to be more influential" and "better communication." What did emerge—particularly in the interviews—was a great deal of dissatisfaction with how organizational decisions were made, and with policies and procedures in general. The group gave many examples where an apparent decision was made but never implemented, or was changed in its implementation. While it was possible to extrapolate specific skills that would improve the process of decision making, our informants focused much more on organizational issues than on those pertaining to individual managerial skill development. If this group had contacted us before we had talked with the president, we would have been pointed in a different direction.

This state of affairs will not surprise the experienced consultant, as it is a fairly common occurrence. But an awareness model based on the interactive Cycle of Experience and around completion of units of work makes it clear that a new unit of work was now required: The conceptions of the top three executives and the group of 25 needed to be shared with all concerned, and an attempt made to integrate these into a common perception of what might be a useful project. Following a report to the top executives of the general findings of the group, several meetings were held with a representative subsample of people. Out of these emerged a design that started with some didactic inputs and exercises for decision making, followed by working sessions in which participants applied their learning to work problems outlined beforehand and brought to the week-long retreat. The design also called for action plans to be made and implemented, with a two-day follow-up several months later. Both individual skill development and organizational concerns were embraced in this approach.

I chose this case because it represents a fairly typical occurrence in organization development consulting. The Gestalt approach is useful in putting the situation in a process perspective, reminding the consultant of his or her role as a helper in generating awareness in the system and in keeping open as to investment in outcomes. Furthermore, consultant presence is a key factor in being able to negotiate work with a complex client system. Unless the consultant can evoke trust in the process and interest in what he or she might be able to teach the group, failure is often the result, and the client system is left with bad feelings concerning how differences can be handled.

Case Two

This is a case in which adherence to my approach resulted in the cessation of a consulting assignment and generated conflict with a client of eight years' duration. The situation and my response to it are not unusual. The case is presented to show that consulting with multiple client constituencies sometimes results in an unsatisfactory outcome. Also, it illustrates once again the need to provide a clear, strong presence. If this is not acceptable in the situation, one learns that further work may not be feasible in that setting.

The case has to do with an assignment for a U.S. multinational corporation. A group executive asked me to do a very sensitive team-building, conflict resolution intervention with the president and key management group in a Latin American operation. The top two executives were U.S. managers sent to this operation; all of the others were native to the country involved. In addition to conflicts between these managerial groups, the group as a whole was very angry about perceived interference from various corporate staff groups. Both the group executive and the president were known to me through previous work in this company, and both felt that I could be of help in this instance due to my previous work in Latin American settings and my knowledge of the firm.

My relationship with this corporation allowed me to deal directly with unit executives in developing assignments, but all projects had to be approved by the corporate vice president for human resources. After several meetings with the executives involved, including a visit to the foreign operation, I negotiated an agreement acceptable to all concerned. I would develop my own contract with the president of the particular operation; this unit would be responsible for my fees and expenses, and I would not render any reports of the work to corporate headquarters. All the parties were pleased with this arrangement.

The ensuing work consisted of fairly standard procedures: individual interviews with all of the local managers; "hanging out" in parts of the operation; feedback of interview data to the top managers; working sessions to improve communication and address problems uncovered; and so forth. Progress over six months was excellent, particularly in getting expatriate and local managers to share more openly with each other, and in beginning to deal with several significant problem areas. All of the managers had experienced moments of being supported and of being confronted by me. Several breakthrough events had occurred and, although there were also some negative experiences, the group wanted to continue our work for an extended period.

At this point I was asked by the corporate vice president of human resources for a report on what was happening. Due to both economic and political pressures, the corporation's chief operating officer had asked for information about this division. I reminded the human resources executive of our agreement that I would not render reports. He said that he was not sure he could adhere to this any longer; his superiors were sympathetic to my position, but felt that I was the best one to advise them on some possible organizational changes involving this operation and its key executives. Pressure was put on the group executive to release me from this restraint and, although he resisted, I could see that he would soon be in an untenable position. I remained firm and said that the only person to whom they should turn for information was the president of the unit. I said that even if he released me to speak, to do so would nullify all the trust I had established with local managers. After several weeks of vacillation, I was told by the president that we would all adhere to the agreement, but the price was that he could no longer engage me to work with the unit.

The major lesson from this experience is that I had neglected an important part of the client system. The fact that we had made an initial agreement should not have been treated as final. It is naive to expect that surrounding parts of an organization will remain quiet during work with a subsystem. Perhaps it was also a mistake to ask that no reports be expected from me. (In other assignments in that firm, I asked that people not tell me anything they did not want repeated, as I would not promise confidentiality.) At any rate my stance was working wonders with the foreign unit but creating a problem at the corporate level.

Case Three

The following case illustrates a situation in which compelling presence may be the only way to reach a difficult client. While this case is not one of organizational consultation, it depicts a moment where the helping professional must act to "grab" a client or lose the opportunity to exert influence.

In a seminar for a group of social workers and related professionals working in agency settings in an industrial city in the Midwest, one of the participants spoke with exasperation about how the Gestalt orientation was alright for middle-class clients or helping professionals, but that it held nothing for people working in social agencies or hospital settings. She told of a recent home visit to a male client who placed a gun on the kitchen table as they commenced their discussion. "See, what good is all your sharing of experience, high contact, and so on, with a gun on the table?" she challenged. I replied that I could see that it was not easy to know what to do at a moment like that, but unless she could find some way to get beyond the gun and "grab" the client, there was no chance to have an impact. I asked her how she felt and what she did. She said that she was scared but that she did not think the gun was loaded or that the client would use it. She proceeded to hold the interview and never looked at or mentioned the gun during it. I replied that this was a reasonable choice under those circumstances, but that a Gestalt perspective opened up some other choices worthy of consideration.

One choice would be to say to the client that the gun had to be put away during the discussion. This would not attack ideology about owning a gun, but would at least make a statement that guns were not part of the relationship with the client. Another alternative would be to ask the client what he was trying to accomplish by putting the gun on the table. Both of these options make the gun foreground, with potentially serious consequences, but they are attempts to make the client deal with the consultant in a more contactful way. Perhaps a safer way would be to get up to leave and tell the client that you will be back when he is ready to talk without the gun. However, this has some risk in that you might return to find the gun on the table again, and having to repeat the procedure of leaving and returning could diminish your power by letting the client see that you can be manipulated.

A fourth choice would be to ask for the gun so that you can hold it while engaged in your conversation. This, too, holds some risk in the potential of upsetting the client by threatening his control. It also might violate your values and boundaries.

It would be presumptuous of me to tell another person what to do in a situation of this nature. However, I do know that the only way of having any impact with this client is through a strong presence that avoids preaching, moralizing, or pretending that everything is fine and that your work together can go on as though nothing has happened. The client most likely has had problems with institutions for a good part of his life, and these responses are standard institutional form. I would do my best, consistent with some regard for my safety, to take a course of action that would compel the client to attend to me. Ideally, I would like to get to the point where I could offer a statement like, "Look, this gun stuff may be OK in other parts of your life, but it is nonsense between us. You have to deal with me. Gun or no gun, you have to talk to me."

Continuing the session without mentioning the gun may be a wise choice—after all, it shows the client that you are not afraid to stay there in the face of it—but more is needed if the client is to be reached at a deeper level.

CONCLUSION

This chapter has focused on the client–consultant relationship, with particular emphasis on expectations and how they are handled. An attempt was made to look at some procedural and structural issues, and at how presence affects the way consultants deal with these. By seeing the job of the organizational consultant as that of continuous negotiation with multiple constituencies, the practitioner is alerted to think in terms of the Interactive Cycle of Experience as a constant frame of reference. One does not engage in a single flow of awareness–energy mobilization–action–completion and closure. Rather, the work may be seen as managing a series of overlapping Cycles throughout the entire engagement. The contrast between psychotherapy and organizational consulting helps to illuminate some of these issues and their implications.

10
Marginality, Autonomy, and Affiliation: The Precarious Balance

The Marginal person
One whom fate has condemned to live in two societies and in two, not merely different, but antagonistic cultures.

Stonequist (1937)

The Marginal Person
Marginality is characterized by personal qualities of neutrality, openmindedness, and adaptable information processing; marginal people thrive on conflict, ambiguity, and stress.

Ziller (1973)

MARGINALITY AND WORKING AT THE BOUNDARY

A basic premise of Gestalt therapy is that change or learning takes place at a boundary between that which is already known or incorporated by an individual or group and that which is not. We say that the real work of any change effort is "at the boundary." The role of the consultant is seen as a boundary role. The effective consultant works at the boundary in that he or she belongs to a group other than the client system. In consulting parlance this is referred to as marginality, and the occupant of the role must function while bridging two cultures and their differing values and norms.

The ability to stay continually at the boundary is extremely difficult. To be effective the consultant must be able to display and use his or her differences while appearing acceptable to the "alien" client system. If one is very much like the system, the consultant–client relationship will be highly confluent. If the consultant is very different, the relationship will be fraught with misunderstanding or conflict. The most useful stance implies a balance; one affiliates with the system yet is clearly autonomous and apart. This provides the consultant with the opportunity to be a powerful force in the client system. It is hard to describe this balance, but it is achieved whenever the following criteria are met:

1. The consultant is seen by the client as being sympathetic and comfortable while working in the system—as fitting in even though a stranger.
2. The consultant's differences are seen by the system as interesting or attractive; the client experiences a compelling presence from another "world."
3. The consultant is fully available to the client but is not a protector or a "buddy."

"Boundary" is a term used to designate the phenomenological moment in which one entity is experienced as separate or different from another. The occurrence of this experience is conceptualized as a line, or a band, or a membrane of demarcation between that which is assimilated by self and that which is not. Boundary is the term we utilize to operationalize the acknowledgment of that with which we are able to make contact and that which we are unable to touch. To have a boundary of any kind is to define or set the limits of interaction (contact) between the individual or system and its environment. Thus if I cannot bring myself to eat certain foods, such as eel or octopus, but I am willing to touch these foods, I have defined a particular boundary between myself and the foods. Likewise, if I am able to experience feelings of anger but am unable to express them I have defined a boundary for my contact with anger. At the larger system level, we can look at how people interact and work together in terms of boundary phenomena. If a member of a group feels that he or she is not listened to when expressing a new idea, or when a member of one group has a hard time getting information from another group, we can describe the nature of these contacts as specific kinds of boundary issues that need not imply anything negative about any of the parties concerned. We merely note the current state of the possible contacts now permitted in the system. Thus boundary is a relational concept that summarizes the state of affairs between reasonably discrete objects or people. If someone says, "I cannot tell where our unit ends and their unit begins," that person is expressing a boundary confusion. Moreover, it is important to see these states as momentary points in a dynamic process, not as fixed structural conceptions. What defines today's state of existence need not be true tomorrow. However, unless the parties involved have some awareness of the boundary they have created, there is no way for them to explore or change it. This is another way of stating the argument that, until awareness of the present situation has been fully heightened, it is not possible to consider changing it.

When we say that learning or change takes place at the boundary, we mean that it occurs through examination of such things as feelings, assumptions, and fantasies, which support the existence of the boundary. It is only by confronting this line—which may be a line of defense or a line of support—and by testing to see if there is any permeability or stretch, that a new experience of the avoided or the unknown can take place. Since this examination is aided by an objective, presumably neutral, facilitator, the marginally positioned consultant is ideally suited to help in its implementation. However, marginal roles are inherently stressful. In addition to the continuous attention required in tracking and supporting the client's multidirected energy system, there are problems of membership group ties, conflicting values, and responsibility for outcomes.

DILEMMAS IN BOUNDARY ROLES

Margulies (1978) has identified three critical dilemmas in behaving effectively in boundary roles: involvement, responsibility, and acceptance. Involvement has to do with the extent to which the consultant becomes enmeshed in the client organization or remains detached. The dilemma here is how sensitive to become to the client's needs and how responsive to be in meeting these needs. One resolution is that the consultant attends to a wide variety of client needs and tries to be aware of all issues with which the system is struggling. At the other extreme, the consultant attends only to the specific, narrow issues of his or her contract. The responsibility dilemma includes the issue of ownership and of which party assumes responsibility for each aspect of a project. A resolution here might involve heavy responsibility for outcomes or goals, and/or acceptance of most, if not all, of the work in a project. Another would be to accept responsibility only for enhancing awareness and to allow action to be the choice of the client system. The dilemma of acceptance relates to personal acceptance of the consultant by the system. One resolution is to maintain minimal personal contact and to be seen as an outsider; another is to become a member of the client group.

Margulies points out that consultant performance in dealing with these dilemmas in a true boundary role requires a constant state of tension, flexibility, and the ability to stay balanced on a middle ground. In dealing with the involvement dilemma, the consultant becomes neither detached nor an advocate, but maintains a delicate balance in which both states may be considered true and not true. Likewise, ownership does not become a big issue; it is dealt with as the need to define a particular responsibility. Acceptance is resolved through being seen as an outsider and becoming, but never achieving the status of, a "member of the family." To achieve these resolutions is very difficult and requires continuous vigilance. This means living constantly with ambiguity and stress, and with many conditions that do not support the values or needs of the consultant. It is not easy to know at each moment what is a helpful intervention and what may be dysfunctional. It requires a good personal balance of tenderness and toughness to care but not care so much that the client system is coddled, or that the organization is left to flounder when some supportive interventions may be needed. Finally, to experience a constant state of aloneness or isolation while in the midst of very engaging interactions with the client requires comfort in the marginal role. None of this is possible without full awareness and understanding of the concept of the boundary role and the way in which change occurs at the boundary. As will be discussed later, it is also important to recognize how the personal needs of the consultant—particularly those for affiliation and autonomy—can interfere with the ability to stay at the margin if they are not managed adequately.

The discussion thus far has concentrated largely on the problems of marginality. A few words need to be said about the positive aspects provided by practitioners of marginal roles. Perhaps the major contribution derives from the need to stay in a constant state of alertness, to remain aware of one's surroundings, and to be ready to move with great flexibility in response to one's awareness. This watchfulness, as it were, and the difficulty marginal people have in becoming assimilated into a modal cultural group, serves to keep them from becoming confluent with a client system. What turns out to be seen as openness to the potential for moving in more than one direction may very well come from a feeling of not belonging anywhere, or from not feeling appropriate when in a fixed position or "pigeonholed" in an easily defined category. To stay in this state of attentiveness requires work, but it results in the development of a finely honed ability to remain continually observant in the face of confusion or possible danger. This is the reward that goes along with the price for living and working at the boundary, and this benefit is not easily achieved.

Three cases illustrate the difficulties inherent in staying at the boundary in ongoing consulting situations.

Case One

This case deals with the general issue of how to work with members of a client system who have significantly different values than the consultant has, or who are disliked because of their personalities, or who are disinclined to act in a way seen by the consultant as essential to the success of the project. In this case I was working jointly with an internal consultant on a project involving a major division of a large company. My internal counterpart did not like the vice president in charge of this division and he made derogatory comments about him to me after some months of work on this project. He avoided contacts with the vice president, spending a great deal of time working with his peers and subordinates, in an effort to "work around" him in furthering the goals of the project. (The internal consultant was well placed in this corporation and reported to the same senior executive as did the vice president.) I watched what was happening for several weeks and then confronted my counterpart with my observations. After drawing out all his objections to working with the vice president, I told him that he did not have the luxury to indulge in his dislike and avoidance of this executive. I worked with him to enhance his awareness of what he was doing, and of the consequences, but I was not at all supportive of any continuance of this behavior. In my view, liking the client executive, or agreeing with his style or ideology, was irrelevant to our work. Either he worked with the vice president—showing him how his behavior detracted from organizational effectiveness and trying to influence him to change—or he dropped the assignment. I was very aggresive in this confrontation, partly because the situation made it difficult for me to reach the executive and partly because I was responsible for the development of the internal consultant. My counterpart was made quite uncomfortable by this confrontation, but his behavior changed very little over the ensuing weeks. As it happened, the vice president left the firm a few months later and with him, that specific issue.

It would be easy to conclude that the difficulty in this situation was that the vice president did not buy into the organization development project—the project being developed by the president and senior vice president of the firm. However, this misses the point. To work at the boundary is to deal with what the client gives you. In this case it meant to keep one's own preferences in abeyance while working with the vice president to get his feelings, assumptions, fantasies, etc., expressed. It means that one cannot remain detached when one does not like something or someone in a consulting setting. It requires talking with the vice president about one's difficulty in doing the job when cooperation is not forthcoming. The truly marginal person should not expect acceptance on any other basis than that working at the boundary is seen to be helpful to the client system.

Case Two

About 17 years ago, my partner and I were asked to develop a major educational intervention for a Fortune 100 manufacturing firm. The goal was to expose a large number of middle-level managers to the changing nature of the workforce, and to teach concepts and methods of participatory management. The top management of the corporation initiated this program as a reaction to motivational and productivity problems stemming from a heavily authoritarian management style. In negotiating our contract, we said that we did not think that this approach in and of itself would be sufficient to bring about significant changes but that we would start here. We stated that while our seminars would enhance awareness of individual managers, much more would be required at the system level for true change to take place. The client executives responded that they would support later programs if we started with the seminars, which was all they thought the system would accept at that time. We agreed, designed and pilot tested the program, and found ourselves with a highly successful seminar attended by about 450 managers during the first full year of operation. During this time we got to know the culture and the people in this organization very well, and we realized that this level of intervention was all that was feasible at the time. We were working at a beginning level of consciousness raising, and the system did not seem ready for more than this.

After two more years of conducting this seminar, we did not feel that the organization was reaping sufficient benefit from the time and money being spent and we initiated conversations about moving on to further steps, such as working with family work groups, and looking at structural and incentive problems. We also submitted a proposal calling for a total evaluation of all the firm's educational efforts and a design of a new program to replace our seminar. We were politely told that our seminar was the best program in the entire corporation—one of the best in its entire history—and that they wanted us to continue doing it for several more years. We ran into a brick wall with regard to consideration of anything else.

The experienced organization development consultant has no doubt confronted this situation at one time or another. Sometimes it is a function of dealing with the wrong level or place in the client organization. In other instances it is a function of being seen only as "educators" or individual development specialists, rather than as organization change experts. From the perspective of working at the boundary, it is important to view our thrust as a test to see if the assumptions, values, and interest of the client might be examined and stretched. We were trying to "disturb a boundary," one we had helped to create when we first accepted this assignment. As a further test of this situation, we could have tried to go around the obstacle we encountered, which would be an even greater disturbance of the boundary. However, we chose not to do so and to continue conducting the seminar. While there were several reasons for doing so (including the fact that we were economically supporting five university faculty and ourselves from this program), this decision took us off the boundary and, in effect, made us part of the client system. Continuing the seminar significantly lowered the potential for change at that moment. One is left with the hope that, by remaining in the system, one will have a later opportunity to test again and to go on to more potent change efforts. If the premise is that change is the option of the client, this is a totally defensible position, but one should not be deluded into thinking that the work will produce significant change. To terminate the relationship with the client would have been more disturbing and might have served to better precipitate the examination we desired. There is no easy answer to this dilemma. (We eventually did several years of intensive team development with one division of the company and my former colleague still consults with certain areas of the firm. The seminars ran for seven more years before being terminated.)

Case Three

A recent occurrence in a year-old, ongoing, team-building relationship with a division of a high-technology firm illustrates the need for continual alertness to boundary issues. Another external consultant with several years' experience in this system, the internal organizational development consultant, and myself, were asked to design an internal education program for a small group of managers who were deemed to need development in specific areas such as financial and business analysis and project management. During the planning of a program of seminars using divisional issues and data as the "cases," two of us expressed reservations about the intervention achieving the change goals desired by the president in requesting this program. Specifically, our concern was that the people now employed in the relevant positions were inappropriate and that even with an intensive development effort, they would not be able to change their behavior in the desired direction. It was acknowledged by all three of us that the culture of the organization would make these changes difficult to achieve, since it valued technical sophistication much more than business acumen. In addition, a recent reorganization had solidified people and structures in a way that would make reassignments a questionable task at the time.

We decided to confront the president with our concern and to test his readiness to look at the issue, even though it meant looking critically at the performance of some managers who were well thought of by him. Our position was simply that we would design and conduct the seminars but that he needed simultaneously to carry out a thorough evaluation of managerial strengths and weaknesses, and to see what his short- and long-term requirements were. This, we said, would involve succession planning and the possibility of bringing in managers from outside the company.

For our present purposes, analysis of this incident in terms of marginality and working at the boundary is more important than the eventual outcome of our intervention. Raising the issue of managerial competence and organizational beliefs about ways of improving managerial performance was the equivalent of saying that we were not satisfied with the assumption that education would solve the problem. As in Case Two, this questioned the appropriateness of the boundary concerning management development and attempted to force consideration of new assumptions and a revised diagnosis of the problem. Defining the boundary at that moment only became apparent by eliciting the president's reaction to our statements and positioning it alongside our response to his response, and so forth. The consultant seeks to define a possible new boundary by disturbing the old.

The difference between this case and the previous one is that, in this instance, we remained in discussion with the president until we achieved an agreement that we would start both the seminars and a procedure for a detailed evaluation of managerial skills and potentials at the same time. We agreed that we would finish the evaluation before the seminars were completed, so that a blueprint for possible changes was in place even if not acted upon until the president was ready to do so. The reader who may see this exchange as a negotiation process will appreciate that negotiation always involves working at the boundary around what is possible in a problem situation. As it turned out later, the seminars were postponed for various reasons, but the succession planning continued to take place.

MARGINALITY AND CONSULTANT STRESS

In the above cases, the consultant moved from a position of relative comfort and stability to one of instability and uncertainty. Immediately before each occurrence, the consultant–client relationship was proceeding smoothingly, supported by agreements or contracts that had been reasonably well defined and accepted by both parties. The questioning of such understandings, whether they are explicit or implicit in nature, is what makes the consultant a force for client self-examination and potential change. But it is a difficult, sometimes risky, business for anyone operating within a marginal role framework to act as a challenger or tester of the status quo. One must cope with rejection if one's questions are ignored or elicit disagreement, particularly if this is a frequent occurrence. It is difficult to weather repeated rebuffs and stay connected to a system of which one is only a marginal member. Inevitably consultants who experience such opposition begin to question their influence in the system and to wonder how to respond. Should one try repeatedly to get the desired client attention? Should one make one or two more tries and then move ahead with a good feeling that the client response reaffirms current readiness estimates? Or should one dig in adamantly and risk losing the client if a desired response is not forthcoming? There are no easy answers or clear guidelines for dealing with this dilemma. Moreover, this is not a one-time, occasional phenomenon in a consulting relationship; it is a basic, periodic occurrence in a dynamic exchange of representatives of two cultures. A competent consultant learns how to manage boundary-testing exchanges, but knows that to do so requires repeated mobilization of energy and the ability to function while being tense or anxious. It comes with the territory to deal with ambiguity and possible conflict on an almost daily basis. As Ziller (1973), Browne et al. (1977), and Margulies (1978) have suggested, marginal roles such as that of external consultant tend to be attractive to people who have an affinity for or become energized by such stress. The trick is to learn how to support oneself while engaged in this role.

DEALING WITH ONE'S MARGINALITY

In attempting to understand the impact of marginality on consultants, it is useful to look at how they manage their careers and how they make job changes. Marginal roles do not typically have the kinds of well-defined and institutional models that are available to socially central roles. This is particularly true for the relatively new role of organization development consultant. As a consequence the task of managing marginality spills out into career dilemmas and a personal search for an ideal way of living and working that is quite different from that which is more generally found in less marginal advisory occupations such as lawyer and accountant. Among the kinds of questions involved in this quest are the following.

- What are the advantages and disadvantages of independent consulting, versus being a member of a consulting group?
- If one practices a marginal role, to what does one belong in a central way?
- How much influence does an external consultant really have?
- How does one achieve a balance between individuality and organizational commitment?
- If one sees oneself as being essentially a private person, what is the meaning of colleagueship?
- If one is accustomed to being a well-integrated member of an organization, does the need for more individuality require going off on one's own?
- Can an internal consultant gain enough marginality to be truly effective?
- Does the internal or external role promise more personal happiness? In which role can one better express who one is?

Preoccupation with these quesitons by practitioners suggests that some degree of stress may be a constant part of their working experience. As indicated, the consultant must care, but not take on too much ownership of the client's problems. Likewise, the consultant must be accepted by the client system but may not become a full member of the system. Working under this tension creates stress, and it would appear that consultants ask themselves the above questions in response to the discomfort of this stress. There are no answers that can eliminate the very real burden of constantly remaining at the boundary in one's work. No possible resolution of such a search reduces the need to use marginality as a powerful force for influence. It may be more fruitful to view the questioning and resultant changes in one's way of working as an attempt to achieve greater support for continuing as a consultant than to view it as a struggle to find a more peaceful or harmonious lifestyle.

What makes the search by consultants for career "rightness" an ongoing concern and worthy of study is that it deals fundamentally with the particular difficulty of those in marginal roles to satisfy this basic need for autonomy and affiliation. While these are universal needs, the consulting role never quite allows for their satisfaction. One does consulting with organizations in order to be attached to some group, but only limited affiliation is possible with a client. In fact, it may well be that the role is chosen largely because one may gain some affiliation while retaining a feeling that the need for autonomy is not compromised in the process. Keeping this precarious balance while maintaining a compelling presence means that while working, one holds in abeyance the full satisfaction of both affiliation and autonomy needs. We can see what happens when this balance is not achieved. If a client relationship is exceptionally good, with mutual warmth and agreement, there is a danger that the consultant will become highly confluent with the system. In some cases this leads to being offered, and accepting, a job with the client firm. If the consultant is overly concerned with maintaining independence and draws very firm boundaries between self and the client, the consultant may be seen as aloof, unsupportive, even alien.

BALANCING NEEDS FOR AUTONOMY AND AFFILIATION

It is worthwhile to look more closely at the definition of needs for autonomy and affiliation as they apply to the consulting role. For shorthand purposes I refer to the need for autonomy as "going it alone," to indicate the strong desire to control one's way of working and one's life-style in general, and to have minimum requirements to make adjustments for the wishes or preferences of others. I refer to the need for affiliation as "going it married," to reflect the strong desire for belonging, coordinated effort, and toward awareness that some degree of personal submission may be advantageous and thus worth accepting. The pursuit of each in the context of professional practice has some clear benefits, as well as a price.

As Table 10-1 indicates, some of the drawbacks of "going it alone" can be remedied through "going it married," and the price of "going it married" can be reduced by "going it alone." From this it is easy to see how sensitive people with high expectations become more in touch with both the advantages and drawbacks of their particular direction just at the time they have achieved a lot by way of satisfying that need. As the rewards are more clearly experienced, so, too, the costs become more painfully apparent.

The push–pull between needs for autonomy and needs for affiliation may be seen in the frequent changes organization development consultants make in their jobs or careers, especially in the movement from internal to external roles. Since 1970 I have noted that a great number of internal consultants and/or related human resource managers left their organizations to become independent consultants after as much as ten to 20 years of experience with only one or two organizations. Perhaps stimulated by the human potential movement of the 1960s, these people expressed growing dissatisfaction with organizational life and a yearning for more individual expression. Many of those who made this move were people who had received a great deal of support from their organizations for professional development, including significant leave for further education and on-the-job work with external consultants. They left at a time when their value to the organization may have been at its highest. About

Table 10-1. The Advantages and Drawbacks of "Going It Married" and "Going It Alone"

	Need for Affiliation (Going it "Married")	*Need for Autonomy (Going it "Alone")*
What it does for you		
	Belongingness	Fewer ties that bond
	Identification with something bigger than oneself	More visibility through uniqueness
	Can do bigger things than one person can do	Can do own thing, be more "eccentric"
	In on overall picture of an organization	Control own time, assignment choice, etc.
	More opportunity to see long-term results	Do not have to check with others or account to many people
	Availability of support system	
Price you pay		
	Must deal with, account to, other people	Possible loneliness; few supports available
	Less control over own time	Must do smaller things
	Decisions must be checked with, and/or approved by others	Creativity limited by own skills and visions
	Commitment (through the "good" and the "bad")	Less centrality to others and to long-term results
	Pressures to conform	Harder to see overall picture

20 of these were people known to me through my work with them and their organizations. Convinced that real progress could not be made without talented internal consultants, I was disappointed in seeing my colleagues act as though the external role was a more satisfactory position from which to practice their profession. But they saw greater possibilities for influence and personal freedom in free-lance consulting. It is interesting to note, in this respect, that these people moved toward roles of greater marginality. According to the findings of Browne and Cotton (1975), external consultants show greater signs of marginality than do internal ones. They also found that the longer an internal consultant remained in this role, the greater was the likelihood that his or her sense of being marginal increased.

While there has been some movement from external to internal roles over the past 15 years, there has been much less change in this direction. Apparently those who change roles are seeking greater autonomy and are less concerned with their needs for affiliation, needs which would seem to be more readily satisfied through being a member of an organization within which their practice is conducted. However, needs for affiliation do not disappear; they must be satisfied in one way or another.

A recent development in this regard is the current enormous interest in networking. A dynamic version of this is to be found in the significant number of networks created by independent organization development specialists—the very people who left organization affiliations earlier—in addition to some younger practitioners who view these people as attractive models. I am familiar with networks in New Hampshire, Boston, Washington, D.C., New York, and elsewhere. In addition, I am acquainted with groups of consultants and groups of therapists from various locales who meet regularly throughout the year for purposes of support, cooperative practice, and career planning. A 1984 conference of consultants and psychotherapists that had networking as its theme drew over 350 participants. It appears that large numbers of people who earlier sought out independence and autonomy now show a deep yearning for affiliation. But even networks serve only as an approximation of full organizational affiliation. It will be interesting to see how needs for autonomy and affiliation are balanced by those involved in them. It may be no easier to achieve a balance in this context than it is to do so in the client–consultant relationship, since network arrangements are simply designs for dealing with marginality. In short:

1. Autonomy and affiliation may be opposing needs but they are not mutually exclusive. To take steps to enhance the satisfaction of one still leaves the satisfaction of the other unfulfilled.

2. These longings are not satisfied simply by how the professional role is defined and practiced. Whether one works alone or as part of a group or organization, these polar needs call out for satisfaction and some form of integration.

3. Actions concerning career and life-style changes may best be understood as responses to heightened awareness of what is missing in a person's life at a given time. Actions may be strongly directed to the achievement of the neglected or atrophied need, or they may be attempts to achieve a better

integration of the two. Thus those who left organizations to develop a more autonomous life may now be seeking networks as a means of attending to dormant affiliation needs.

Several examples provide further insight into these conclusions:

1. In 1968 I left a consulting firm I helped to start (in 1955) because I realized that the organization had grown to the point where its needs and the interest of my partner were interfering with my own interests. Within two years I made two different affiliations with other consultants, both of which provided colleagueship yet preserved a great deal of my independence. At the same time, I gave up the leadership of the Gestalt Institute of Cleveland and helped to design a new format of governance that allowed me to stay connected but freer of organizational burdens. Neither of these moves was made from a base of the clarity I now have, but in retrospect they show a desire to retain affiliation and yet have the experience of greater individual freedom.

2. In 1963 I became part of a group of professional people who developed their own community property of 16 townhouses. All of the adults involved in the project wanted to give up their traditional, more isolated, single-family living pattern. Yet the most important factor in the development of the community was that of designing the housing so as to ensure privacy for each family. Needs for affiliation and needs for privacy seemed to be equally important to this group of people, which included five psychologists, three business executives, two physicians, a dentist, five university professors, a lawyer, and an architect.

3. Though Fritz Perls was a restless man who moved around a lot and who became famous for his independence and his ability to "do his own thing," he left behind strong, viable groups of helping professionals in at least four cities in which he conducted training workshops. At the time of his death, he was working on the development of a "Gestalt kibbutz" in Canada.

IMPLICATIONS

Starting with a definition of working at the boundary and of the dilemmas of those who occupy the marginal role of the consultant, the discussion has proceeded to examine how organization development consultants deal with their needs for autonomy and affiliation. This analysis shows that the pull of these needs shapes the search for role definition and satisfaction. Since it is difficult to satisfy these needs fully in marginal roles, changes in jobs or ways of working are seen as a reflection of the consultant's longing at a given time for either more affiliation or more autonomy. The burden or stress of working at the margin may very well be too much to tolerate without some kind of personal adjustment from time to time. In this regard it is interesting to note that those practitioners who make role changes and those who make no major change in their way of working both report periodic concern with the issues raised herein. The key to understanding career concerns lies not in choices made but in the recognition of the difficulty in working in marginal roles for extended periods of time, and the need for balance in life.

It follows, then, that the question of whether the internal role or the external role is the best one, or whether it is best to practice alone or within a group of external consultants, does not get at the crux of the problem. One can work at becoming part of a network just at the time of becoming a one-person independent consultant. The person who is well affiliated may want to find space for more autonomous pursuits within the organization of affiliation as an alternative to leaving and becoming an unaffiliated consultant. But to work at the boundary means to attach oneself to an organization while at the same time remaining separate. None of these choices removes this requirement while one is engaged in an actual consulting assignment. From this perspective, the struggle with needs for affiliation and for autonomy may be seen as one way of understanding marginal roles and the price one pays for working at the boundary. From concern with these needs the highly aware consultant can learn something about marginal roles. One of the insights to be gained from this awareness is that personal needs can only be satisfied outside of relationships with client systems. To work at the boundary means to bracket or hold in abeyance the quest for full satisfaction of needs for affiliation and for autonomy. The positive side of this state is that it is just this tension that makes the consultant a powerful force.

REFERENCES

Browne, P.J., and Cotton, C.C. "Marginality, a force for the OD practitioner." *Training and Development Journal*, vol. 29, no. 4, April 1975.

Browne, P.J., Cotton, C.C., and Golembiewski, R.T. "Marginality and the OD practitioner." *Journal of Applied Behavioral Science*, vol. 13, no. 4, 1977.

Margulies, N. "Perspectives on the marginality of the consultant's role." In W.W. Burke (ed.), The Cutting Edge: Current Edge: Current Practice and Theory in Organization Development. San Diego: University Associates, 1978.

Stonequist, E.V. *The Marginal Man.* New York: Scribner's, 1937.

Ziller, R.C. *The Social Self.* Elmsford, N.Y.: Pergamon Press, 1973.

Epilogue: Learning to Deal with Regret

All moral stances possess an immoral option.
Meron Benvenisti (1986)

The experienced observer of organizational life cannot help but notice the strength of forces devoted to the attainment and maintenance of "correct" ideology, "successful" strategy, the "best" policies and procedures, and so forth. Whether it is in the realm of economic philosophy (are we a free market system or a planned economy?), or planning and strategy (what businesses, markets, structure should we select?), or the realm of ethics (what practices are appropriate for obtaining business or for being socially responsible?), there is a strong thrust to find the one "right" answer. Despite the knowledge that we live in a very complex, pluralistic world, the manager's quest often is based on the assumption that the world is made up of binary phenomena, and that bipolarity is the nature of things: there is a right solution to every problem and other solutions are wrong—there is a right philosophy and there is a wrong philosophy. This orientation may well be supported by a universal cultural drive to achieve a workable, transmittable system for dealing with problems of internal cohesion and of adaptation to the external environment. Insofar as each organizational unit is a cultural unit, a task of its managers is to develop, maintain, and transmit that system most appropriate to the survival of the unit.

Given this, it follows that a great deal of managerial time and effort are devoted to monolithic thinking: if the right ideology, goals, and methods can be determined, it is presumed that actions that follow from these basic values will reveal a world exhibiting uniformity or an harmonious pattern. Managers generally think and act as though this ideal state is possible once proper stances have been achieved with regard to basic values and assumptions. How else can we account for the intense feelings that go along with the need to be right? These feelings are often so strong that their expression goes beyond mere rightness to that of righteousness. Attitudes and actions become imbued with a sense of virtue and moral justification. Once having decided upon *the* way of dealing with a problem, the manager acts as though it is the only right way and believes that all other solutions, as well as those who believe in them, are wrong.

If the world were this simple, there would be no problem. But reality dictates otherwise, as should be clear when we consider that philosophy, strategy, and policy almost always develop out of the weighing of alternative choices, very few of which have all good features and no undesirable aspects. However, as movement is made toward a choice, energy is mobilized around the good features of that choice and the positive aspects of the alternatives being rejected are given less attention. The opportunities inherent in the rejected choices are lost or minimized, as are the negative aspects of the action selected. This can lead to righteous adherence to the choice. The experience of regret, which would follow from full realization that certain actions preclude other desirable courses, is also lost.

RIGHTEOUSNESS: THE ENEMY OF REGRET

Regret stems from an understanding that every strategy or policy simultaneously carries with it some benefit and some cost. It derives from the awareness and acceptance of responsibility for selecting an alternative that has some bad features and rejecting an option that has some good features. Righteousness—the enemy of regret—makes this state of awareness difficult to achieve. The simultaneous experience of both pleasure and sadness in making the choice is lost. While the joyful side is more readily accessible, righteousness makes it unbearable in such instances for the manager to feel sorry, to be remorseful about what has happened, or to mourn what has been lost. The experience of regret is thus denied and managers are left only with the potential for the defensive devices of projection or, in rare instances, feelings of guilt. Projection acts to place the negative aspects of the decision outside one's system and to lodge them as the responsibility of the external world. Guilt serves to place the undesirable aspects within one's system and places responsibility or blame on self rather than other. In managerial circles guilt occurs less than projection, for to experience it would be an admission of weakness. Projection is the more common reaction in support of righteousness: If one is right, the other must be wrong. In any event, neither allows for the truly awesome recognition that is the experience of regret.

I consider the difficulty of bearing the awareness of regret to be one of the great barriers to organizational change, as well as to individual change. A compelling task of organizational consultants is to teach managers what regret is, and how they may learn to be more effective in a pluralistic, uncertain world if they can allow the experience of regret into their awareness. To do so attacks righteousness at its very roots, and is far more effective than attempts to loosen its power by offering the rhetoric of countervailing positions (other "righteousnesses"). Gestalt therapy and other existentially oriented approaches provide much value here through:

- Emphasis on awareness and the here and now experience.
- Focus on the process of decision making rather than content or ideology.
- The concept of creative indifference and the integration of polarities versus absolutist thinking.

It should be understood that I am talking about experience *at the moment of decision or action,* not the realization that might come when the later consequences of the action are manifested. While the dynamics of regret may be the same for both moments, true learning or derivation of useful meaning from the total experience will be much greater if it is supported by initial experience of what is lost and what might be gained through the decision or action. In this respect it is interesting that the Japanese use the term "to choose" to indicate those actions Westerners refer to as "to decide." Perhaps Eastern philosophy better recognizes the push-pull relationship between righteousness and regret; in choosing, there is an implication that all choices have their positive and negative features. One might well feel some regret or remorse as well as some satisfaction in every instance of choosing. Consultants to managerial decision-making processes, such as strategic planning or task-oriented team development, can be of great help here by guiding managers to consider remorseful aspects in greater depth than is customarily afforded to this side of the equation. This is an important example of what we mean when we say that an important task of the consultant is to help the client be fully aware and responsible for actions stemming from awareness.

In order to understand the concept and experience of regret, it is important to understand the process of action taking arising out of righteousness. This process can be best illuminated by what are seen as "big acts," those actions that stand out as being strong, forceful, and provocative in nature. Examples of "big acts" include significant reductions in workforce; mergers, acquisitions, or divestitures; structural reorganization (e.g., formation of the Saturn organization by General Motors); changes in managerial philosophy or style (e.g., going from autocratic to participative management). The issue is not whether any of the actions taken are appropriate or correct, but what kind of organizational learning takes place as these actions unfold. To use the terminology of Argyris and Schon (1978): Does single-loop or double-loop learning occur? As each stage of the decision-making and implementation process unfolds, is it possible for new awareness to emerge that might lead to reconstitution of basic values and assumptions, or does righteousness prevent this from occurring and merely allow for remedial action or a "Band-Aid" solution?

THE PROBLEM OF ASSAULTIVE PROVOCATION

The big act is even better understood if we look at the level of broad social change. In recent years we have been bombarded by the media with stories that describe provocative acts engaged in by various groups that are highly dissatisfied with progress in bringing about changes they desire. The hijacking of TWA Flight 847 and the cruise ship *Achille Lauro* are classic examples of this, as are the car bombings and assassinations we hear about with alarming frequency. These kinds of actions are not confined to long-term international conflict situations. Attacks on birth control clinics, raids on animal research laboratories, and intensive, almost vicious, lobbying efforts that defeat or significantly modify legislation stem from a similar kind of righteousness. Harassment, ugly picketing, firesetting, and general vandalism have been reported in over 20 birth counselling centers in the past three or four years. Bill Baird—a leader of the pro-choice movement—has received so many threats against his well-being that he is living apart from his family, which is hidden from public view (*New York Times*, January 6, 1985; January 12, 1985; January 29, 1985; September 1, 1985). Responding to a different issue, in April 1985, a group calling itself the Animal Liberation Front kidnapped more than 700 research animals, stole documents, erased computerized data, and vandalized the psychology and biology laboratories of the University of California, Riverside. This was only one of such actions carried out in the United States and Canada in recent years (Cunningham, 1985; Sperling, 1985). It is important to note that animal laboratory raiders and pro-life fighters are generally responsible members of their communities.

The perpetrators in these cases reflect a growing tendency in the world to excuse actions and their consequences by adopting an attitude of righteousness. All that is "right" is attributed to themselves by those taking such steps, and all that is "wrong" is attributed to the targets of the actions—and to those who do not understand the righteousness of the perpetrator's causes or fail to help them get what they want. My thesis in these concluding remarks is that the Gestalt Cycle of Awareness is a useful framework for understanding the phenomenon of righteousness, and that an important task of the consultant is to help client systems to become aware of its manifestation in organizational life and of its consequences.

Typical explanations as to why people engage in such severe actions invoke hypotheses of denial of wrongdoing, or elaborate rationalizations that the means justify the ends. A more useful way of looking at the process preceding such actions proposes that so much energy is attached to the awareness of the perpetrators that it must be released through action. Their awareness is so "supercharged" that action bursts forth in a manner that may be analogous to sexual orgasm. As people experience frustration in all walks of life due to the growing difficulty in achieving consensus in a divergent, pluralistic world, we are likely to see more and more manifestations of righteousness. But righteous acts tend to produce righteousness on the part of the targets of these actions. Unless those who act out of righteousness can learn to experience regret in giving up less extreme alternatives as they enter into these actions, there is little hope that the energy can be discharged in more effective ways. There is an inverse relationship between regret and righteousness; the stronger the experience of righteousness as the springboard for action, the less it is possible to experience the often painful burden (the awareness of regret) that there is a negative aspect to a seemingly appropriate action, and that other possible approaches to the problem may be irrevocably discarded.

The tragic element in the foregoing examples is not simply that they are acts of assaultative provocation that are harmful to others. The "supercharged" energy that results in these actions develops over a period of time, a period during which energy could be discharged in smaller actions from which wider awareness would follow. The major problem with intensely focused action steps is that awareness is narrowed considerably as energy to act builds up. This lessens the potential to see alternatives or to feel fully responsible for both the good and the bad in the actions taken.

The focus thus far has been on the perpetrators of the "big act." However, it is equally important that, at the time of the actions, the targets also experience regret for actions taken or not taken in the past or present. Without this there is no opportunity for joining of the multidirected energies of all the people involved. If both sides of the animal research or abortion issue can realize that there is good and bad in what they are doing, there may be some hope for actions that deescalate the conflict even if they are not a total resolution.

One of the problems in operationalizing a way of dealing with the issues raised herein lies in the very nature of the "big act." These actions take place because people lack appreciation for and/or the competence to take the effective smaller steps that would make up a process of incremental change. The small steps of incremental change discharge energy and serve to broaden or expand awareness. Supercharged energy leads to actions that are supported by high energy and limited awareness. If one can act before energy becomes too much to contain, smaller actions will take place and there will be less of the unfinished business that festers until an explosion occurs. The aggregated learning from numerous small steps makes it harder for people to remain fixed in bipolar thinking, since this tends to produce awareness of more alternatives and to reduce adherence to rigid dichotomies of good/bad or right/wrong. The Gestalt Cycle of Experience emphasizes completion of small units of experience and focuses on incremental discharge of energy. The aim of the Gestalt-oriented consultant is to help client systems to use the energy that derives from awareness in a process of incremental change. In this sense what is presented in this book applies mainly to situations in which the beginning contract between client and consultant contains a modicum of agreement that learning at the awareness level is important to foster improved organizational functioning. This is not a blueprint for revolutionary change.

IMPLICATIONS

Though less striking in intensity than the described social issues, the search for correct actions and proper ideology leads to many actions by managers that may momentarily alleviate a problem situation but in the long run prevent organizational learning from taking place. We are all capable of righteousness when we are frustrated in getting what we want.

We can make this discussion more specifically relevant by looking at an increasingly common managerial "big act": the down-sizing of organizations in mature industries or other businesses in severe economic straits. Typically a decision to downsize comes about when awareness around the organization's problems is highly charged. The top managers of the firm experience a crisis or see potential disaster ahead. Declining sales and profits, increasing costs, and other aspects of the competitive environment appear as intransigent problems unless a drastic step is taken. From this follows the ideologically "right" conclusion: We can only survive by having fewer employees; for the good of the many, the few must pay a price. The very term "down-sizing" illustrates the search for language that will allow the bad aspects of the desired action to appear more palatable. The practice of layoffs (perhaps supported by a time-worn concept of labor as a commodity) is deeply entrenched as a management procedure. Layoffs have been with us for a long time. Recently early retirement has become a version of the practice.

In some cases layoffs may be the only viable action. They do have the advantage of eliminating significant fringe benefit costs as well as direct salaries. However, some firms choose different options, for instance, seeking cuts in wages for all employees or various other alternatives (Perry, 1986). In either case the experience of regret would derive from full awareness that choosing one approach precluded the other. The morality in not firing anyone may carry with it the immorality that certain individuals may have to work harder in order to carry marginally productive people. In the case of layoffs, the immorality in causing the debilitating effects of unemployment is balanced against the morality of protecting the interests of stockholders and the majority who remain employed. To choose one option is not to choose the other, and managers must act to preserve their organization in difficult times. The process leading to the decision should be rich in awareness of all the aspects of the choices, with a complete acknowledgment of what is gained and what is lost. This allows for true ownership of the choice and what is good and bad about it. Rather than adhering to rigid ideology, this process fits in with the criteria for educated problem solving. By simply assuming that top management should make the decision, and that the right decision is to do a layoff, there is no space for development of full awareness around all the possible choices.

This example deals with the "big act" that appears to be required when energy builds up and must be acted upon through strong, stern measures. Ideally the highly aware organization will track its problems and take smaller actions as it goes along, so that it is not placed in a crisis mode. There is growing appreciation of this in the increased environmental scanning activities to be found in many firms. But even given the benefits of such endeavors, in an uncertain, seemingly uncontrollable, and complex world, widened awareness should lead to the recognition that no action is without some cost or damage to someone or something. Yet managers must act. The consolation is that there be some benefit in the actions chosen. The mature individual or organization makes the best choice it can and experiences regret while doing it. Having made the choice through a rich process of awareness allows for the choosers to experience fully both the joy or pride that comes with the good aspects of the decision and the sadness that comes with recognition of its bad aspects. This is difficult to accomplish when an impending crisis necessitates the implementation of the "big act." For this reason, the more complex the problem and the greater the number of people, interests, and perspectives involved, the more important it is not to get stuck in trying to find the grand solution. A rhythm of awareness-energy-action-closure built around smaller units or incremental changes is much more manageable.

CONCLUSION

While this discussion has been somewhat general, and guidelines for tactical responses by consultants are not clearly delineated, the message I want to convey is not difficult to grasp:

1. The process of deciding to act is one of choosing among alternatives which contain both positive and negative features.
2. The building up of energy to act out of righteousness drives people to take strong actions that are not supported by a rich awareness process allowing for the experience of regret at the moment an action is chosen.
3. The experience of regret is the full awareness and ownership by those who choose an action that contains nega-

tive aspects and precludes other actions that have certain positive features.

4. Without the experience of regret, it is difficult to achieve true organizational learning; people will act out of limited awareness, remain fixed in their righteousness, and overcertain about the actions they have chosen.

Two important implications derive from these premises. The first has to do with how consultants deal with the client's process. It suggests that consultants maintain an ever-vigilant concern with the client's awareness process, with how much and how well all aspects of the situation are experienced during the sequence of choosing and acting. This means to stand firm for, and to make a case for, the value of detailed attending to the rhythm of awareness and energy when client systems face a difficult problem or decision.

The second implication relates to the consultant's own process. Consultants may also have a problem dealing with their righteousness and lack of awareness of regret. When one becomes enamoured with, or an advocate of, certain techniques or methodologies, there is a tendency to apply these to most problems that clients present. A case in point would be to see all motivational problems yielding to the solution of structural rearrangements, such as job redesign. Even more troublesome, potentially, is when consultants develop a strong value or ideology, e.g., a bias toward participative management and involvement of members of the client organization in a drive for empowerment. The message here is not that consultants must give up their preferences. Rather, it is that consultants will be better able to act on their values if they are fully aware of the negative aspects of their chosen path and the positive features of the rejected choices. For example, the attempt to achieve a highly participative management group can well lead one to support actions to mute the impact (modeling and setting of expectations) of a highly charismatic leader. But, if one is aware of and appreciates the transformational aspects of such a leader, one may assist in the development of a participative solution that embraces the positive aspects of such leadership.

By engaging in an extensive awareness process that attends to both positive and negative features of available alternatives, consultants are able to act wisely rather than dogmatically. Only through this process can the experience of regret mollify the influence of righteousness.

REFERENCES

Argyris, C., and Schon, D. *Organization Learning: A Theory of Action Perspective.* Reading, Mass. Addison-Wesley, 1978.

Benvenisti, M. *Conflicts and Contradictions.* New York: Villard Books. 1986.

Cunningham, S. "Animals stolen, facility damaged in break-in." *American Psychological Association Monitor,* vol. 16, no. 6, June 1985.

Perry, T.L. "Least cost alternatives to layoffs in declining industries," *Organization Dynamics,* vol. 14, Spring 1986, pp. 48–61.

Sperling, S.E. "I was violated," *American Psychological Association Monitor,* vol. 16, no. 6, June 1985.

Index

About the Author

Edwin C. Nevis, Ph.D., has more than thirty years of experience as an organizational consultant. During this period he has also been associated with the Gestalt Institute of Cleveland as a faculty member and as President (1960-1971). Dr. Nevis teaches at the Sloan School of M.I.T. where he has also served as Director of the Program For Senior Executives. He is the Editor of the Gestalt Institute of Cleveland Press.